Fatal Error

Fatal Error

THE FINAL FLIGHT OF A NAVY WWII PATROL BOMBER

Gary D Cooper

Copyright © 2015 Gary D Cooper
All rights reserved.

ISBN: 150616059X
ISBN 13: 9781506160597

Eternal Father, Strong to save,
Whose arm hath bound the restless wave,
Who bid'st the mighty ocean deep
Its own appointed limits keep;
O hear us when we cry to Thee,
For those in peril on the sea.
The Navy Hymn

Dedication

To the memory of the eleven U.S. Navy warriors who bravely fought and sacrificed their lives for their country and the three valiant crewmen who survived this mission against all odds.

And to the memory of the courageous Australian Z Special Unit warriors who risked their lives in an attempt to save the U.S. Navy flyers and the three Z Special Unit heroes who sacrificed their lives while trying to save the lives of others.

May their bravery and sacrifices never be forgotten.

Table of Contents

            The Crew··xi
            Introduction··xiii
Chapter 1 Near Lalombi, Celebes, Dutch East Indies··············1
Chapter 2 Selecting the Crew···3
Chapter 3 San Diego, California··16
Chapter 4 Kaneohe Bay, Territory of Hawaii·······················21
Chapter 5 Hawaii to Tawi-Tawi··32
Chapter 6 Tawi-Tawi, Philippine Islands······························41
Chapter 7 Attack on Sandakan Harbor·································50
Chapter 8 First Long War Patrol···56
Chapter 9 Along the East Coast of Borneo···························67
Chapter 10 Near Lalombi, Celebes, Dutch East Indies············78
Chapter 11 Under Attack··86
Chapter 12 Rescue at Sea··91
Chapter 13 Operation Raven, the Search for the Missing Crew·····102
Chapter 14 In Custody of the Kempei Tai·····························109
Chapter 15 The Execution···119
Chapter 16 End of the War···124
            Epilogue···131
            Acknowledgements··135
            Notes··139
            Bibliography··151

The Crew

Patrol Plane Commander	Lieutenant DeLand Joseph Croze	Minneapolis, Minnesota
1st Pilot and Navigator	Ensign Marshall Henry Hicks, Jr.	Columbia, South Carolina
2nd Pilot and Navigator	Ensign Lewis Albert Wheeler	Michigan City, Indiana
Flight Engineer	AMM1 John Patrick Igoe	Brooklyn, New York
Flight Engineer	AMM2 Daulton Clifton Stephenson	Mercer, Tennessee
Flight Engineer	AMM3 Broadus Lyle Bumpas, Jr.	Memphis, Tennessee
Deck Gunner	AOM3 Kenneth James Crow	Ossian, Indiana
Bow Gunner	AOM3 Joe Harvey Garcia	Corpus Christi, Texas
Tail Gunner	AOM3 Dale Aaron Hunt	Kokomo, Indiana
Waist Gunner	AOM3 Charles Watson Moorfield	Kenbridge, Virginia
Senior Radioman	ARM2 Owen Douglas Huls	Columbus, Ohio
Junior Radioman	ARM3 Edward Adley Calhoun	McKeesport, Pennsylvania

Guest Riders from USS Pokomoke (AV 9)

Meteorologist	AerM2 Donald Milton Pell	Brazil, Indiana
Machinist	AMM2 Robert Bernard Jezewski	Milwaukee, Wisconsin

Lewis Wheeler's Navy Suitcase
(Photograph taken by the author)

INTRODUCTION

The Suitcase

BETTY MORRIS LOOKED OUT THE front window of her second floor apartment in Michigan City, Indiana, onto the street below. It was May 1994, the house had been sold and her downstairs neighbors had just moved out that morning. She looked at the mound of boxes and bags left curbside for the trash and spotted something unusual. It was a medium-sized olive green suitcase in good condition sitting among the items left for the trash man.

That looks too good to throw away, she thought. I could paint flowers on it and use it for decoration. I'd better not take it now, though. They may remember it and come back for it. But if it's there tomorrow morning, it's mine. She continued packing in preparation for her own move in two days.

As she backed down the driveway the following morning on her way to work, Betty spotted the suitcase. Three houses down the street, the men on the garbage truck were banging trash cans and yelling to one another. Betty took a look around, grabbed the suitcase, and threw it into the trunk of her car just as the garbage truck pulled up. "Two more minutes and that suitcase would have been gobbled up," she said with a smile as she drove off.

The following Saturday morning, sitting in her new apartment, Betty remembered the suitcase she had forgotten about in the rush of getting packed and moved. She brought it in and placed it on her dining room table. When she opened the suitcase, she was amazed to find that it was filled with photographs, letters, documents and memorabilia of a handsome young naval officer named Lewis Wheeler. Letters and telegrams reported his status as "missing in action" and later told of his death in combat during World War II. Betty had no idea who Lewis Wheeler was until she saw a wedding photograph. Even though the wedding had been fifty years ago, she recognized that bride. It was Betty Jean, her downstairs neighbor. She had married Lewis just before he went overseas. He never returned. Although they had been high school sweethearts, they were married only a few brief days before Lewis shipped out. Betty Jean remarried shortly after the end of WWII.

Betty Morris put the suitcase in her closet for safe keeping. When her son, Tom Bunton, relocated from Indianapolis to San Diego, Betty gave him the suitcase, urging him to take care of it. Tom became my neighbor and good friend. He kept the suitcase in his closet, and although I had been in his home many times, he never mentioned it.

I retired in 2001 and moved away from San Diego. Tom and I stayed in touch, and I visited him each time I was in the area. One day in April 2009, I visited Tom when his mother, Betty, was there. After lunch, Betty said, "Tom, why don't you show Gary that suitcase." Betty knew I was a retired navy commander and thought I might be interested in seeing what was in it.

Tom dragged out the suitcase and put it in front of me on the dining room table. I looked carefully at each document in the suitcase, piecing together in my mind the life of this man and his short career as a navy pilot. He had received both the Purple Heart and the Bronze Star, so I knew he had put up a strong and brave fight before losing his life. I saw a photograph of his crew and looked into the faces of those young men. Most were just teenagers or men in their early twenties looking eager to do their part to win the war. Not a single one appeared apprehensive he might not return.

I was lost among those documents that had taken me back to 1945, to an era I barely remembered as a child. Finally I looked at Tom and Betty. "What do you plan to do with this suitcase? It's much too valuable to leave in the closet."

They both agreed they would like to have it returned to the Wheeler family, if someone who remembered Lewis was still alive. Tom was a busy attorney and didn't have the time to take on that kind of research. Betty admitted that she had no idea where to begin.

"I'll do it," I said. "I have been doing genealogical research for years and with my military background, if there are relatives alive who remember Lewis Wheeler, I will find them."

Tom and Betty agreed, and I made copies of everything in the suitcase. I began my search as soon as I returned home. The first thing I did was to build a family tree using precious little information in the suitcase about his family. I knew Lewis was from Indiana. I had his wife's name and saw that his father's name was Bert. In just a few days I found a Bert Wheeler in Kokomo, Indiana, and with information discovered online, I built the family tree all the way back to the American Revolution, only to discover I had chosen the wrong Bert Wheeler. It was painful to toss that entire family tree in the trash, but it was the wrong family.

I finally found the right Bert Wheeler and his family. They had moved to Gary, Indiana, where both Bert and his wife had found employment. Census records listed all their children's names, and I found the obituary for Lewis Wheeler's sister. It listed her next of kin that included her daughter who lives in Florida. I found her by using information on the internet and then called and spoke with Jean Eggleston, the niece of Lewis Wheeler.

Jean was cautious at first, thinking it might be a scam, but when she realized I did not ask her for any information about herself and only told her about her uncle, she was delighted. "Lewis Wheeler was the hero of our family," she said. "My mother talked about him every day of her life until she died." Jean told me she has a photo of Lewis holding her when she was a baby. "He was a beautiful man, an all American golden boy. He was very popular, and everyone loved him."

I picked up the suitcase from Tom, flew to Florida, and returned Lewis Wheeler to his family.

Back home, I felt satisfied. I had done the task I set out to do and brought it to a successful conclusion. But I couldn't stop looking at the faces of those boys in the crew, wondering who they were and what happened to them. Every one of them had a story and had loved ones just as Lewis Wheeler did. I started looking for them, one at a time.

It was an amazing journey with frustration followed by elation when I found a family. All of the families were happy to know someone had remembered their loved one and was telling their story. I received photographs, letters, and details of their lives from many of them.

During the early phase of the search, I found a man who lived just an hour from me who was researching the same crew. Jim Carter, a nephew of crew member John Igoe, responded to an e-mail I sent him, telling me he was recuperating from open heart surgery. We exchanged the information we both had and within three months, Jim passed away. I continued my search with a woman from Australia, Sally Olander, whom Jim had met on-line. Her cousin was an Australian Army man who served in the famous Z Special Unit, a top secret organization trained in espionage that operated behind enemy lines in the most dangerous operations in the war. That cousin, John Whitworth, lost his life when the Australians sent a team into enemy territory to search for the missing American crew. Sally cheered me on and celebrated with me each time I made a new find. I honor her for the superb work she did that helped discover the final resting place of her beloved cousin more than sixty years after his death.

I wanted to get as much of the story as I possibly could. I acquired from Jim Carter, before he passed away, a copy of the official war diaries of the navy squadron to which the crew was attached. From the National Archives in Washington, DC, I obtained over five hundred pages of the War Trial Records. A trip to the National Archives branch in St. Louis, Missouri, gave me over a thousand pages of the military service records of each crew member. I needed to know what the men looked like, their eye and hair color, their height and weight. I looked for anything that could bring that photo of them to life, right down to marks and scars on their bodies. I wanted to know them.

I am not sure the research will ever end, but at some point you have to say, I have enough. It is time to start writing. I have told the story to the very best of my ability, adding dialogue and situations that could have happened, based on my experiences during thirty-five years of active duty in the navy, serving as both an enlisted man and a commissioned officer. If I have misrepresented any member of the crew, it is my fault and mine alone.

Gary D. Cooper
Commander, U.S. Navy (Retired)
Palm Springs, California

CHAPTER 1

Near Lalombi, Celebes, Dutch East Indies

June 5, 1945

OWEN HULS GAVE UP THE possibility of sleep. He looked at his watch. It was 5 a.m., and the eastern sky had just begun to turn orange and yellow in anticipation of sunrise. Most of the men were still lying curled on the sand in a pretense of sleep. The eerie sounds of the jungle, just a few hundred yards inland, had kept the crew on edge throughout the night. Except for an hour or two when he thought he might have dropped off to sleep, Huls had stared into the darkness wondering what the next day would bring.

He had been looking and listening for one of the PBM-5 Mariners their squadron promised would come to their rescue. But no plane had appeared. Their situation was worrisome. Huls knew that Japanese occupied many of the islands. In the half-light of early morning he studied the area. He wasn't sure what to make of the three native canoes beached near a line of coconut palms. Somebody was undoubtedly around.

Huls got to his feet and stretched. He saw their skipper, Del Croze, standing near the water's edge, gazing down the beach at their seaplane that was now partially resting on the sand in the low tide. Huls trudged through the loose sand toward him. "Where the hell do you think those rescue guys are?" said Croze as he approached. "Shoulda been here by now. Jezewski died last night. We couldn't get the bleeding stopped. Do you think there's enough juice to power up the transmitter again?"

"I don't know, sir. It's worth a try." Huls hiked on down the beach to the Mariner. Looking at the plane's heavy damage in the morning light, he was once again amazed that they had been able to reach this island. He clambered up the ladder to the forward hatch and worked his way to the radio room. He was glad he had his flashlight. It was too dark to see much. Too bad about Jezewski, he thought. He didn't know him well, had only talked with him at breakfast the day before on the Pokomoke. But he seemed like a good guy.

Huls powered up the transmitter and receiver and checked they were tuned to the ground-control frequency guarded by the USS Pokomoke. He picked up the microphone and put on the headphones but heard nothing. Not even a crackle. "Pokomoke Ground Control, this is Mariner 062 - over." Nothing. He repeated the call several times. "Any station this net this is Mariner 062, come in please." Only silence. Shining the flashlight on the power meter, he saw the problem. The batteries had discharged during the night. He yanked the headphones off of his head and threw them across the room. They bounced off the radar equipment and landed at his feet. "Shit!" he yelled.

Making his way back to the hatch, Huls clambered down the ladder. Croze was no longer in sight. As Huls started up the beach, he heard voices coming from the direction of the mangrove trees and reeds that stretched inland. He ducked behind a nearby palm and crouched down. His heart started pounding when he saw eight armed Japanese soldiers walking toward the plane. He had never felt life-threatening fear like this before, and it crept up his spine then down his body leaving him almost paralyzed. His vision seemed to narrow.

CHAPTER 2

Selecting the Crew

October 4, 1944

The journey that left Del Croze and his crew stranded on a Pacific island in fear for their lives had begun months earlier at the U.S. Navy base in Banana River, Florida. None of the crew who arrived at the base in the fall of 1944 thought of themselves as exceptional men. They came from a variety of middle and working class backgrounds. They were to receive navy training that was standard for all recruits during the war years. Yet they went on to live and die heroically. The story of their ultimate sacrifice is a tribute to the courage and endurance of these men as individuals and also as representatives of thousands of others who fought in the Second World War.

Meet The Crew

Owen Huls was very young, just six months out of high school in Columbus, Ohio, when he joined the navy. A member of the Hi-Y club, a boy's service club, in high school, he was likely an idealistic young man. During his navy years, he sent home a significant percentage of his salary each month to assist his mother with household expenses. By the time Owen Huls arrived at the Banana River base, he had already won a Combat Aircrew badge while flying on smaller PBY seaplanes in Jacksonville. But like the rest of the trainees, he had no real combat experience.

Owen quickly bonded with his new crewmates as they converged on the base. At first these men were like himself, just guys from somewhere, with brief accounts of where they had come from and what they had been doing. Ensign Lou Wheeler, fresh from flight school, rode in by bus from Pensacola on October 4, 1944. A native of Michigan City, Indiana, he had lived in several places including a few years in Elizabethton, Tennessee, where his father owned a country club, and then during the depression, in Lake Helen, Florida. More recently, the family had moved back to Michigan City to live with Lou's grandparents.

Lou liked telling how on the bus he had met fellow officer Marshall Hicks and discovered that Marshall had graduated from flight school just one day before he had, although he had been given an earlier date of rank of September 16th. Lou said, "I told him it looks like you are senior to me by about twenty days. And Marshall came back with, 'Well, Lou, I'll try not to make you stand at attention for too long when you talk to me!'" Lou grinned. He liked Hicks. He was a southern boy who grew up in Columbia, South Carolina, and later lived in Arcadia, Florida, where his dad got a job as a stationmaster for the railroad.

"It was in the middle of nowhere, a hundred miles south of Orlando," said Hicks. "I was sure glad when we moved back to Columbia. We bought a small dairy farm, and I ran it myself until I went away to college."

Near the end of October, Owen met the four Aviation Ordnancemen who arrived to begin a training class in Mariner PBM seaplane weapon systems. At first they were just names: Kenneth Crow, Joe Garcia, Dale Hunt, and Charles Moorfield. Kenny Crow told Owen how on the day he reported for duty Ensign Wheeler inquired why he had dropped out of the flight training program at Purdue University. "He asked, 'Was it the mechanics?' I told him, 'No, as a matter of fact I'm pretty good at mechanics. I rebuilt the engine on my 1937 Plymouth. Maybe it was the hand-eye coordination I just didn't get.' Anyway, he assured me that the main thing was that I had done well in the ordnance school in Memphis."

Marshall Hicks (Top) and Lewis Wheeler (Bottom)
(Official U. S. Navy Photographs)

Owen was particularly interested in getting acquainted with Aviation Radioman Third Class Edward Calhoun, who had just reported aboard. He was to serve as the junior radioman of the crew, while Owen, with his Combat Aircrew badge, was the senior radioman.

Rounding out the crew were the Aviation Machinist's Mates, Daulton Stephenson and Lyle Bumpas.

Not until late November did the men have a chance to meet their skipper, Lieutenant Del Croze, the man who in a few months would fly them into the war zone. His reputation had preceded him. DeLand Croze, better known as Del, had been the star end of the University of North Dakota football team and captain of the wrestling team. After graduation in 1938, he had joined the navy reserves and later in 1941 was appointed an ensign. The men heard he had spent two years on the USS Humbolt, a seaplane tender, stationed in Brazil, where their seaplanes sometimes had to bomb German submarines prowling the coast. But as for actual combat service, the men concluded, Croze was probably as green as they were. When they received a summons to attend a meeting with Croze, who had just arrived on the base, all were curious about the man who would head their team.

Croze was sitting on the corner of his desk waiting for the crew. He was feeling tense and hoped it didn't show. This was his first command assignment. A lot was at stake. Headquarters was demanding that his men be ready to ship out to the Pacific in just a few months. He got to his feet to shake hands with each of the men as they filed into the room and approached to introduce themselves. God, they're young, he thought. That Garcia looks like a high school kid. Maybe it's just because he's short. He'd heard that Garcia was a Golden Gloves champion boxer. Hopefully, he was up to the job. This wasn't going to be some high school sports camp.

DeLand (Del) Croze
(Compliments of Mel Mattsen)

"Good afternoon, men," Croze said, after the crew had settled into their folding chairs. "I'm glad to have a couple of days with you before I return to Corpus Christi for my last two weeks of training. Then I'll be back here full time. We have a lot to accomplish. Fortunately, I've been getting good reports on your day and night training flights in the PBM aircraft. We are ready to step it up now.

"First, here's what is at stake. When you get to the Pacific, you can expect twelve-hour patrols. They'll be exhausting and hard. You'll need to stay alert at all times. We have lost a lot of planes. Your survival depends upon knowing your jobs and your plane thoroughly. When you have a Jap Zero coming at you, you don't have time to stop and think about how to react. The PBM-5 is a great plane, but it's complex and things can go wrong. That's when you do some flying by the seat of your pants. You have to really know your plane—what it can do and what it can't. One man's mistake can hurt the rest of the crew or damage the plane."

Croze paused. The room felt stuffy and unusually warm for November. But as he scanned the crew, he felt reassured they were listening. He glanced at the faded portrait of Commander-in-Chief Franklin Roosevelt on the far wall and continued his speech. "Tomorrow we're going on a simulated twelve-hour patrol. We depart at 0700 and fly to Guantanamo Bay. We'll have a senior pilot and three senior instructors to observe all of us, both in the cockpit and in your positions throughout the plane. On the return flight, I want as many of you as possible to change positions. You never know when you'll need to take over somebody else's job in an emergency."

Croze explained that he expected the radiomen to take turns operating the plane's radar equipment. He asked co-pilot Ensign Wheeler to trade jobs with the navigator, Ensign Hicks, and told the machinist's mates, Stephenson and Bumpas, to take turns as Flight Engineer. Finally, he said, "You four ordnance men—you are going to have the most essential jobs of all when we enter combat. Consequently, I want each of you to spend at least two hours at each of the five gunnery positions. There won't be ammunition, but you can operate and rotate the turrets.

"The flight is approximately six hours for each leg of the trip. We'll be on the ground in Guantanamo for an hour. I've arranged for hot meals to be delivered there since our galley won't be operational. Are there any questions?" The room was silent. "Well, okay then. You are dismissed. I'll see you all on the plane at 0700 tomorrow morning, ready for takeoff. Get a good night's rest."

After the men left, Croze sat down behind his desk and stared out the window at the unpaved parking lot. He felt satisfied the guys would be decent to work with. He hoped he wouldn't lose too many of them. The navy didn't talk much about it, but he knew the statistics. With worn equipment and inexperienced crews you never knew what would happen. He heard some of the men outside laughing as they headed back toward the mess hall. He hoped they'd keep up their good spirits.

Early the next morning after a breakfast of bacon and eggs, the men started trekking toward the boats that would ferry them out to their seaplane. It looked like good flying weather. The morning was cool with a slight haze that should soon lift. Off-shore, the PBM was bobbing in the light chop, rising and falling at its moorings like a large, dark bird.

"So, what do you think, Stephy, are we ready for this?" Bumpas asked. As senior enlisted man at that time, Stephenson was the designated crew chief.

"Sure. Hey, we've been doing good. Don't let the skipper scare ya."

"Just wish they'd let us go ashore. Get some rum and cokes and hoochie coochie with some of those Cuban señoritas," said Dale Hunt.

"In your dreams, Hunt. Two rum and cokes and we'd be carrying you back to the plane," said Owen Huls. "You wouldn't even get close to a señorita."

They were all feeling pretty good. Today would be a chance to prove what they could do. Although nobody talked about it, they were proud to have been picked to crew a PBM-5.

The Martin Mariner PBM-5 Seaplane

It was a huge plane called a "flying boat." When compared with the popular B-17 and B-24 bombers, the PBM-5 exceeded their wingspans by five feet, their over-all length by five feet and their height by eight feet. With its two 2,100 horsepower Pratt & Whitney R-2800 combustion engines and four-blade steel propellers, it could attain speeds of over 200 miles per hour.

Although crews complained the plane was under-powered, they appreciated its patrol range of over 2,000 statute miles, considerably more than that of the more popular PBY seaplane. The men heard that the plane was proving to be a reliable craft for reconnaissance, anti-submarine warfare, and bombing missions in the Pacific theater of the war. It also had great success in rescuing downed pilots. The bomb load was a respectable 8,000 pounds. Bomb bays were located in the rear of the engine nacelles.

Graduation From Banana River

On the flight to Cuba, the crew lived up to Croze's high expectations. They arrived back at base tired from a long day cramped in the plane but confident they could handle their jobs. The senior pilot and instructors congratulated all of them on their performances.

The next day, the men began aerial gunnery practice. Every crew member, regardless of their primary job, had to become a proficient aerial gunner. Hitting a moving target from a moving platform was no easy feat, they quickly discovered. But by the end of the course, their instructors pronounced all of them competent with aerial weaponry. Joe Garcia was awarded the prized bow turret gun position based on his top scores in the gunnery training class. Croze gave the deck turret gun position to Kenny Crow, the second highest scoring crewman in the class. He assigned Charlie Moorfield to the waist hatch guns and Dale Hunt to the tail gun position.

Graduation day for the Banana River PBM-5 trainees was January 2, 1945. They cheered, gathered for a group photograph, and then ran to pack their suitcases and sea bags. They were headed for leave—fourteen whole days of it plus five days travel time. Fourteen days in which to enjoy family and friends for one last time before reporting to the Naval Air Station, San Diego, on January 20th. After that they would be shipping out to their war zone in the Pacific.

LAST TRIP HOME

The men crammed months of living into two short weeks. Lou Wheeler got home just in time for his wedding to the girl he had been dating since the tenth grade. His bride, Betty Jean Zeismer, had the arrangements complete. All Lou had to do was to show up at the altar. They were married on January 6, 1945, in St. Luke's Lutheran Church in Michigan City, Indiana. Lou's brother, William, was his best man. After the ceremony, Betty Jean and Lou drove sixty miles to Chicago for a wedding dinner in the Walnut Room of the famous Bismarck Hotel, where they would be spending their wedding night.

Lewis and Betty Jean Wheeler and the Wedding Party
(Photo from suitcase found by Betty Morris)

Marshall Hicks was rushing home to his bride, Betty. When Marshall and his fellow officer, Lou Wheeler, first met on the bus en route to the Banana River base, they had fun discovering that each had a girlfriend named Betty. They both agreed they were ready to get married. Marshall, however, suddenly decided the time for marriage was not soon—but now. Five days after arriving at Banana River Marshall announced he was not waiting until their leave in January. His big chance came when he learned that the start of classes in the Aviation Training Unit was delayed until more enlisted men arrived. With his buddies cheering him on, he caught a military hop to Charleston Army Air Base, about one hundred miles from his home. On October 9, 1944, Marshall Hicks married Betty Belcher. He was twenty-one years old, she was eighteen. Betty moved in with Marshall's parents while he returned to Florida.

When Marshall finally got back home in January, two weeks of leave time proved too short for these long-separated newly-weds. As he was packing his suitcase for the trip to San Diego, Betty determined she could not let him leave again without her. They had no idea where they would find a place to live but decided to worry about that when they got there. They boarded the Greyhound bus together.

Up in Minneapolis, Del Croze's wife, Elsie (née Peterson) was making a similar decision. She had married Del several years before, on March 16, 1941, the day he was appointed a navy ensign. But with only two weeks of leave in January before his departure to the Pacific, Elsie was not ready to give him up. She took a leave of absence from her job as a school teacher and joined him for the three-day train trip to San Diego.

Charlie Moorfield had a wonderful surprise when he stepped off the bus in Kenbridge, Virginia. His older brother, Alva, along with his sisters, was standing there waiting for him. Charlie had not dared hope he would have a chance to see him on this leave. Alva had joined the Navy three years

Joe Garcia and Leo Gonzalez
(Compliments of Richard Garcia)

before, right after the attack on Pearl Harbor. Charlie thought he would be away on his Pacific battleship where he was serving as a gunner's mate. But Alva requested a leave so he could be home with Charlie. The whole family made the most of their reunion, not thinking about the possibility that it could be their last.

Joe Garcia spent time with his girlfriend, Mary, went hunting and fishing with his buddies along the Nueces River in Corpus Christi, Texas, and got to know his baby brother, Richard, who was just four months old. He liked talking to him: "Hey, little brother, are you gonna remember me when I come back from the war? I'll take you fishing with me and teach you to be a boxer like your big brother." He gave the kid a fake punch in the nose and got a big smile in return. Joe's best friend, Leo Gonzalez, wanted a picture of Joe before he left for the war. Joe did not have one to give him, so they went down to the local photo studio and had their picture taken together.

Eddie Calhoun's family postponed Christmas until he got home so they could all open their presents together. "We had lots of snow, and I got elected to shovel the driveway every morning," he told the men later in San Diego. "Guess I won't be doing that for a while."

Daulton Stephenson said that he helped his dad rebuild the tractor so it would be ready for spring planting and also helped their preacher fix the church roof. "The rest of the time my wife, Jewel, and I visited with family and friends," he said.

With home, family, and leave behind them, the men made their way to San Diego to complete their training. When they arrived on Saturday, January 20, 1945, each one checked in with the Officer of the Day and was sent to the barracks with orders to report on Monday morning to the headquarters of Patrol Bombing Squadron 98, located in a nearby building on the Naval Air Station. That first evening back, the men sat around until after midnight telling stories of their time at home. They tried to keep their stories light and funny and not think too much about the sadness they felt when they left home, knowing they would not return until after the war, if at all.

Back row: Lyle Bumpas, Lewis Wheeler, DeLand Croze,
Marshall Hicks, Daulton Stephenson
Front row: Joe Garcia, Dale Hunt, Kenneth Crow, Charles Moorfield, Owen Huls,
(temporary crewman J. Dewey) and Edward Calhoun
(Photo from suitcase found by Betty Morris)

CHAPTER 3

San Diego, California

❦

January 20, 1945

THE DAY AFTER THEY ARRIVED in San Diego, some of the men were grumbling. Their training sessions were not to begin for two days. "Crap, we could have stayed home one more day," Hunt complained. "I was just getting friendly with a girl I thought I had a chance with."

"Knock it off, Hunt," Bumpas said. "I plan to catch the water taxi into San Diego and look around. If any of you guys want to come with me just meet me here at 6 p.m."

No one heard the officers griping. They were enjoying the good housing options available in the area. Lou Wheeler received a room with a view of San Diego Bay in the bachelor officer's quarters.

When Del Croze checked in, he was told that he was eligible to stay at the Del Coronado Hotel, not far from the Naval Air Station. Part of the hotel had been set aside for officers and their wives. "Hey, honey, how about this - just like a holiday," said Del as they carried their luggage into their room with an ocean view. The sun had just set behind Point Loma when he and Elsie took a walk on the beach. The water and sand were beautiful, although the concertina wire stretching along the beach at water's edge and the presence of armed sentinels interrupted the vacation fantasy they were enjoying.

Hotel del Coronado, San Diego, California
(Photo taken by the author)

After spending the first night in a small hotel on El Cajon Boulevard, Marshall Hicks and his wife Betty spent the weekend looking for a place to stay. They finally found a room in a large home at 5141 Marlborough Drive in the Kensington section of the city. Betty and Marshall lived there until he completed his training, and she returned to South Carolina.

Any thoughts of holiday fun disappeared for the men on Monday morning when they mustered at the headquarters of Commander Fleet Air, West Coast, commonly referred to as COMFAIRWEST. As they looked over the outline of training that would be conducted for the next two months, they saw that the primary emphasis would be on aerial attacks on surface ships and submarines, surveillance, bombing, and mine laying.

What they found most interesting was the news that they would soon be taking delivery of a brand new PBM-5 Mariner, Bureau Number 59073, fresh off the assembly line. In early February, Croze, accompanied by Wheeler, Stephenson, Bumpas, and Huls, flew on a C-47 transport plane to Naval Air Station Corpus Christi in Texas to get their plane. Before the bare-bones crew of two pilots, two machinist's mates, and a radioman started their twelve hour flight home, they had to learn about the many upgrades on the PBM-5. Acclimating to the new plane proved challenging. The crew back home spent a few days flying the plane before they were comfortable with all of the changes. The new Mariner would remain their plane until they arrived at their final destination of Patrol Bombing Squadron 20, located at Tawi-Tawi Island in the Philippines.

The crew's remaining time in San Diego proved strenuous. They trained for long hours almost every day, making simulated attacks on ships and submarines as they departed San Diego harbor. They dropped practice bombs near the ships and threw hand grenades at submerging submarines who then reported the closeness of the blast. They also bussed to Camp Elliot in the north end of San Diego for small arms practice. They trained alongside marines at the rifle range in order to qualify with the M1 rifle and Colt pistols.

Despite the work, most of the crew members loved the time they spent in San Diego. Weekends were free, so they headed for town. San Diego was bursting at the seams with thousands of service men walking the streets day and night. It had taken on a carnival-like atmosphere. Most of the men went to Mission Beach to stroll along the boardwalk and ride the Giant Dipper roller coaster at Belmont Park. Some were attracted to Balboa Park and the Zoo.

Kenny Crow and Eddie Calhoun took the Greyhound bus to Long Beach to go to The Pike. During WWII the area became a magnet for active servicemen. It was a huge amusement park very popular with the sailors who went there for two reasons - girls and the roller coaster, a huge wooden dual-track coaster built on pilings over the water. They rode the roller coaster three times, walked along the board walk, looked at all the arcades, bought hot dogs at the food stands, and enjoyed a few of the smaller rides, but with the crowd's being mostly sailors, they did not meet any girls.

Fatal Error

Owen Douglas Huls
(Compliments of Maryanne Huls Dardarian)

Owen Huls, who grew up in Columbus, Ohio, had never seen the Pacific Ocean. He asked Bumpas to go with him to the beach. They rode the water taxi to San Diego and a local bus to the beach. Taking off their shoes and tying the laces together to carry them over their shoulders, the two men rolled their uniform pants up to their knees and stepped into the cold surf. "My feet are frozen, let's get out of here," Huls said after wading for half an hour. "I promised my girl and my mother I would send pictures of me in my dress blues. Let's stop downtown and find a photo studio." They caught a bus to the foot of Broadway and walked up the street. Photo shops were not hard to find. There was one in every block with employees on the sidewalk trying to convince sailors to come in. They settled on the Pierce-DeWhit studio where Huls had his picture taken. He returned the following week, picked up two photos, and sent one to his girlfriend and one to his mother.

Just before the end of their training, the officers went to a party at the Hotel Del Coronado. Hicks brought his wife, Betty. Croze's wife, Elsie, had departed a few days earlier to resume her job as a school teacher. Wheeler came alone. Del Croze was the life of the party, wearing his normal lieutenant bars on one collar and a chaplain's cross on the other, giving humorous and inappropriate moral advice to the officers and their wives.

On April 4, 1945, the crew completed their training in San Diego. Next stop was Hawaii.

CHAPTER 4

Kaneohe Bay, Territory of Hawaii

April 5, 1945

DEL CROZE TAXIED THE PLANE away from Coronado Island and took off a few minutes past 0200 on the morning of April 5, 1945. Lou Wheeler, the navigator for the first half of the flight, had plotted the course and estimated flying time to be just over sixteen hours. The early departure from San Diego was needed to make a day time landing at their destination of Kaneohe Bay, on the northeastern side of Oahu, Territory of Hawaii.

The previous day, Del Croze had gathered his crew together. He was happy with their progress and how they jelled, working together as a single fighting team. He addressed the men. "I'm really proud of the success you men have achieved in your training here in San Diego. I expected you to do well, but you did even better than I had imagined. Early tomorrow morning we will leave the United States and head for our last training area before entering the war. Keep up the good work, men, and I know you will be able to handle whatever may happen when we meet the enemy face to face. As you may have heard, our navy, marines, and army ground forces have begun an attack on Okinawa. The battle is important. It's the closest our ground forces have come to mainland Japan so far in this war. Our air strikes are already having a major impact. As you have likely heard, last month, on March 10, incendiary bombs killed approximately 85,000 people in northern Tokyo. Let's hope we can get this war over fast and get back home."

After four hours of smooth flight, the men were relaxed and quiet. The silence was broken by an announcement from Eddie Calhoun at the radar station. "Radar to Pilot, heavy weather dead ahead, range about 20 miles."

"Pilot to all stations - make sure your harnesses are properly fastened and any loose gear is stowed for heavy weather, we have a thunder storm ahead that we are going to try to avoid." Croze made a course change to get by the storm. As they skirted the edge of the storm they hit an area of violent turbulence. The plane dropped 50 feet and a wing dipped hard to port. The plane began to shake. Within five minutes they were out of the turbulence and back into clear skies. Croze checked with the crew to see if there were any injuries. Other than a couple of bruises and a cut on Garcia's head, there were no serious injuries.

By mid-afternoon the cloud-capped mountains of Oahu came into view. In the bow turret, Joe Garcia was amazed by the beauty of the islands. He had never seen anything like this in his life. His thoughts were interrupted by an announcement: "Radar to Pilot, incoming bogey dead ahead closing fast." A fighter plane patrolling around the island came out to challenge the incoming PBM-5. Wheeler turned on the Identification Friend or Foe system and an exchange of codes confirmed the PBM-5 to be friendly. The fighter pilot waved from his cockpit and returned to his patrol.

As they neared Kaneohe Bay, Croze requested permission to land. Using the last three digits of the Bureau Number of the plane as his call sign, he radioed for permission to land. "Ground control, this is Mariner 073, request landing instructions." Ground control responded and advised Croze to make his approach on 225 degrees. During their descent, the men crowded the windows for views of the base. They wondered what kind of condition it was in. Croze had told them how the Japanese strafed and bombed it, destroying the whole fleet of PBY seaplanes, just minutes before they opened up on Battleship Row in Pearl Harbor on December 7,

1941. The base had been in existence for only a year when the attack nearly demolished it. From all appearances it had been substantially rebuilt.

The men were relieved to get on the ground. After over sixteen hours in a plane that reeked of aviation fuel, they couldn't wait to get out of their flight suits and into a hot shower.

In the morning after breakfast in the chow hall, they arrived at the training office a few minutes before 8 am. The office was bare except for a desk in the front, a chalkboard on the wall, and a dozen folding chairs scattered around the room. A tall slender sailor with light brown hair was writing on the chalkboard. He turned around to face the crew.

"Hey, look who's here - our favorite Irishman!" Stephenson yelled as he stepped forward to shake hands with the sandy-haired sailor, John Igoe.

"Good day to ya. You blokes must be knackered after that long flight," Igoe said to the crew in his soft Irish brogue.

John Igoe, an Aviation Machinist's Mate First Class, had been a popular instructor with the crew both at Banana River and in San Diego. He had taught the machinists how to become flight engineers and was one of the instructors who examined the crew on their training flight to Guantanamo Bay. He had completed his tour of duty as an instructor, and when time came to return to an operational unit, the navy approved his request to join Croze's crew. Igoe had arrived at Kaneohe a few days earlier to help set up the final phase of the crew's training. He was an expert in teaching the PBM systems and a very welcomed addition to their team.

Igoe explained the plans for the month that included simulated land attacks as well as continued practice on surface ships and submarines. The men spent the rest of the morning unpacking their sea bags and stowing their gear. Wheeler insisted that Garcia go to sick bay to have the cut on his head checked. It was Kenny Crow's 22nd birthday, but he kept it to himself.

About noon, the four ordnance men went into Honolulu to see the sights. "Hey guys, this is Hotel Street," Moorfield said. "My brother, Alva, was here a couple of years ago and told me there are a bunch of whore houses on this street. He said they charge two dollars for two minutes."

"What the hell can you do in two minutes?" Garcia asked.

"Well, Alva said that after being at sea for six months, two minutes were all most of the guys needed."

The men couldn't find any whore houses and checked with a Shore Patrolman they saw on a corner. He told them the government had closed them down about six months ago. "Sorry, guys, you're out of luck."

They ate lunch at Wo-Fat Chinese restaurant and ordered the chop suey special. After lunch they took the bus to Waikiki. The beach was lined with concertina wire at the water line and swimming was not allowed. There were no sun bathers. After walking on the beach for a few minutes, they stopped at the Tiki Bar. "Chattanooga Choo Choo" was playing on the juke box. Moorfield asked for a Pabst Blue Ribbon. "Sorry, sailor, all I have is Royal and Primo." They all settled for a Primo. Hunt lit a cigarette and then offered Moorfield a light.

A sailor was sitting at the bar. "Hey, you guys just roll into town or something? Everybody here knows they don't have Pabst Blue Ribbon."

"Yeah, we just landed yesterday. Our PBM-5 is over at Kaneohe," Moorfield said. "How long have you been here?"

"Longer than I wanted to be," the sailor responded. "I was here when the Japs attacked."

"Holy shit, what was that like?" Garcia asked. "I remember when that happened, but I was just fifteen years old in the ninth grade. That seems like it was a long time ago."

"If you had been here, sailor, it would seem like it was just yesterday. It's something I'll never be able to forget. I dream about it all the time."

"What was it like? I've seen a few news reels of it, but I can't imagine what it was like to be here," Kenny Crow said.

The sailor motioned for the bartender to bring him another beer and lit a cigarette. "Well, let me tell you, it was pure hell, that's what it was. I was in the barracks, right across from the submarine headquarters, sound asleep. A few minutes before 0800 my bunk started moving around and a nearby blast knocked me on the floor. Somebody yelled, 'It's the Japs! They're bombing us!' We all threw on our clothes, grabbed our rifles and ran outside. I could see those bastards making dive bomb attacks on the ships. We started firing at their planes, I don't know if I hit one or not. One plane flew so low, the pilot looked over at me, smiled and waved. I didn't smile back, but I did wave - with just one finger. We all turned and fired at him.

"Just about then, the Arizona went up like fireworks. The whole ship seemed to lift up then settled back down on its side. The concussion almost knocked us down. Guys were jumping into the water that was covered with burning fuel. I yelled to the guys with me that we needed to help those poor men swimming in the fire. We ran down to the water just as three other navy guys were starting out in boats. We all jumped in the boats and headed for the men in the water."

The sailor lifted his beer bottle and drained it. When he put it down on the bar, the guys noticed his hands were shaking. He nodded to the bartender for a refill. "The first guy I got to was completely black with oil, but I could see that his hair had all burned away. I grabbed him under his arms and pulled him into the boat. The skin on his arms was peeling off. He couldn't say anything. He just gasped for air for a minute and then died. He was just a kid, maybe eighteen or nineteen years old. Maybe about your age," he said, looking at Garcia, who always got remarks about youth since he was short.

"We kept helping those guys in the water until we got 'em all out. The Japs finally left about 0930. Almost every ship in the harbor was burning and some were sunk. The Japs had plans to attack the Philippines, Singapore, and Hong Kong and didn't want the US to interfere so they destroyed our navy and destroyed almost 200 airplanes at Hickam Field, next to Pearl Harbor. We lost nearly 2,500 Americans that day and about half that many wounded. Let me tell you, I'll never forget that day. Dead people all over the place, children and adults crying and screaming. We got our butts kicked by those Japs, but we're kicking their asses right now."

Garcia nudged Kenny Crow and nodded toward the street as three beautiful Hawaiian women in grass skirts walked by on their way to a hula show. The sailor frowned momentarily, took another sip of beer, and continued. "It seemed like a well planned attack but for some reason they didn't hit our huge oil reserves. It would have put the navy out of business for years if they had bombed that. They'll wish they never made a move on us, I'll guarantee you that. Now you know why the president called it a day that will live in infamy."

The sailor sat staring into space for a few moments and then said, "Well, you guys are young. Hope I didn't bore you with all that. My wife says I talk too much about it. And she's right. It's history. You won't likely have to go through anything like that. War's going to be over pretty soon."

"You think...?" said Garcia, as he got to his feet. "We've heard the Japs are toughing it out."

"Yeah, you're right. But they can't last too much longer. Hey, you guys want another round before you go?"

"No," said Kenny. "We gotta get going. But thanks. You can tell your wife we liked the story. Kind of reminds you what the hell we are all doing around here." The men shook hands with the sailor and then caught a bus to Pearl Harbor. They needed to see the place now, after knowing more about what happened there.

When Del Croze departed the plane on Saturday noon, he set off, not to town, but to meet his brother Bert at the front gate of the base. It was great seeing him. They gave each other a big hug. "You're looking good, big brother," said Del. "The business life must be agreeing with you."

"Yeah, we're doing all right," said Bert. "Even after three years, they still have plenty of construction work for us around here - thanks to the Japs."

Dressed in khaki trousers and a bright aloha shirt, Bert stood eye to eye with his 6'2" brother. Although the two brothers looked a lot alike, Bert had dark brown hair and hazel eyes, and Del had auburn hair and blue eyes. Bert and his family had moved to Hawaii in 1939. He was a construction engineer, and his company won a contract to build reinforcements at

Pearl Harbor, including new ship repair facilities and the large fuel storage tanks that survived the attack on Pearl Harbor.

The two brothers had seen each other only on occasional visits when Bert had business on the mainland. Now, with his whole month on the island, Del was looking forward to spending every weekend with his brother and his family. By the end of his stay, he had fallen in love with Hawaii. "You know, Bert, after the war Elsie and I are going to live here. This is like living in paradise." Del hesitated, thought for a minute, and then looked at his brother. "If anything happens to me in the war, I want to be buried here in Hawaii. I mean it, Bert. Please promise me you'll make that happen."

"Oh, come on, Del, don't talk like that. You'll be back after the war, and you and Elsie can be our neighbors."

"Promise me, Bert, I mean it."

"Dammit, Del. All right, I promise."

On Monday, April 9, 1945, the crew began their final month of training, following the schedule Igoe had posted. Just three days into their training, the men were given the sad news that President Franklin D. Roosevelt had died. Harry Truman was the new president. The men admired President Roosevelt and believed his leadership was a major reason that America and the allies were winning the war. They did not know much about Truman, some had never even heard of him, but they hoped he was up to the challenge.

The month passed quickly as the men honed their skills until they were considered ready to face whatever they might encounter in the war. With departure imminent, however, their feelings were conflicted. The excitement of going off to engage the enemy was tempered by homesickness after Croze reminded them that they had better get their letters home written and mailed before they left Hawaii. From here on, he said, the mail service might be less reliable.

Kenny Crow bought some U.S. Navy air mail stationery at the exchange on May 7th and sat down at a table to compose a letter to his sister. He carefully placed some lined paper under the thin page on which he was writing and began:

Dear Sis,

Just received your letter this evening & was quite surprised to hear that I have another nephew, and what's his name, may I ask? All good people are born in April you know?? To [sic] bad it wasn't the Sixth, then I could have someone in the family to celebrate my birthdays' with. I got a letter from Pauline yesterday, and she asked about you. Did Dad have anything new to say when you seen [sic] him. I get about 3 or 4 letters a month from him. I guess he's quite busy though. So you got a new watch uh! I think it was about 14 years ago when you got your last wrist watch wasn't it?

"Who ya writin' to? Your mom?" Kenny looked up from his page. It was Stephy, holding a cup of coffee.

"Oh, hi….no, well, she's almost mom - my sister, Helen. My mom died when I was six years old, and my fourteen-year old sister took over the job of raising me. That was probably a pretty rough job! Actually, I guess you could say we pretty much took care of ourselves. My dad was real busy farming and working on the highway. Sometimes I went over and stayed at my cousin Junior Eichhorn's house. They were good folks – told me their door was always open."

"Wow, that's tough. I didn't know all that. Sorry."

"No, it was okay. My sister and I were always close. She's got a new kid, now."

Stephy paused, then said, "Well, I'd better let you finish. I'm supposed to be writing home, too, but darned if I can think of anything new to say. We keep pretty much doing the same stuff. They get mad, though, if I don't write. See ya in the morning."

"See ya, Stephy." Kenny picked up his fountain pen again.

I asked Pauline to write you a line & give you the latest, if she understands what I mean. I suppose the headlines to-nite made you feel quite good. V-E Day? Well sis I really can't think of much to say, that I can say, so I guess I might as well

close. Oh! Yes, I'm still in the best of condition and when you answer this letter, change the address to VPB 20 don't forget like I did.
>*Well*
>>*So Long*
>>>*&*
>>>>*Goodluck As Ever*
>>>>*Ken Crow*
>>>>>*P.S. Your letter made it in 3 ½ days.*

This was one of the last letters Ken's family ever received from him. His father later reported receiving one from him written on May 31 with a promise to write again in four days. Unfortunately, that would have been the date of the crew's final patrol.

On Wednesday, May 9, 1945, the crew gathered outside the training office. With sea bags packed and training completed, the men were preparing to leave Hawaii and begin the journey to their new base of Tawi-Tawi in the southernmost part of the Philippine Islands. They were about to exchange Hawaii's tropical paradise for a war zone, and the crew was nervous but anxious to go. The men were standing around talking and smoking cigarettes, waiting for the skipper.

When Del Croze arrived, John Igoe called the men to attention. Croze briefed the crew on the current status of the war. "Good morning, men, perhaps you may have heard this already, but yesterday, May 8th, President Truman announced that Germany has surrendered to the Allied Forces. The war in Europe is over, but it's a much different picture here in the Pacific. Japan is determined to fight to the last man and remains a strong and dangerous enemy. Our part in this war has not changed. We will need to face the enemy with strength and courage until the war is won."

He also briefed the men on their route across the Pacific Ocean from Hawaii to Tawi-Tawi. The long trip would take ten days with stops for refueling and a full day of rest at Johnston Atoll, Kwajalein, Saipan, and Jinamoc Island. Owen Huls groaned inwardly when he heard how many days they would be stuck on the roaring, vibrating plane. At least the first day's trip, to Johnston Atoll, would be short – only five and half hours.

Ken Crow and his sister Helen
(Compliments of Donna Bradburn)

"Plan to depart at 1100 hours," said Croze. "As soon as the plane is fueled, the ground crew will move it onto the apron, and you will be able to load your gear. I know this month has been difficult with a very demanding training schedule. I hope you were all able to take advantage of the weekends to enjoy this beautiful island. Right now you'd better get to the Navy Exchange if you need any last minute toilet articles. Be back here no later than 0930."

The men returned to the training office in time to watch their plane being towed to the apron. As soon as the ground crew had detached the tow rope, they went aboard with their sea bags and stowed them in the crew's berthing compartment. Pre-flight checks started at 1000 hours. Huls made radio contact with Ground Control. Croze checked with Wheeler, who was navigating that day, to make sure he had the charts that showed the dredged lanes for seaplanes at Johnston Atoll. Satisfied they were ready to go, Croze and Hicks completed all the checks in the cockpit. Igoe was at the flight engineer position and on signal from Croze, he started the engines. Croze got clearance for takeoff and taxied down the ramp and into the bay. He waited while the ground crew removed the temporary wheels. With special permission to fly over Pearl Harbor, Croze dipped the wings as they passed over the sunken hull of the USS Arizona. The men observed a moment of silence in honor of their shipmates who lost their lives on December 7th.

CHAPTER 5

Hawaii to Tawi-Tawi

May 9, 1945

AT 1530 HOURS JOHNSTON ATOLL came into view. Croze landed the plane and taxied to nearby Sand Island, a short distance to the northeast from the main island where the seaplane lanes had been dredged. They found a post close to the shore where they could tie up the plane. Ground crews soon arrived to refuel the plane and to ferry the crew members ashore in small boats. It felt good to get off the plane. The men went to the barracks, a large room with cubicles, each containing four bunks. A separate room in the same building was set aside for the officers. Croze, Igoe and Stephenson stayed aboard the plane.

Sand Island had beautiful white sand beaches littered with sea shells and lined with coconut palms. After dinner the men left their flight suits in the barracks and walked barefoot along the sands in the warm, humid air, wearing only their boxer shorts. Garcia found an old sock abandoned on the beach and filled it with sea shells. Perhaps he intended them as souvenirs to take home to his family someday. They would be found later among his possessions when they cleaned out his locker. Huls and Bumpas stripped off their boxers and dove into the water. After some encouragement that the water was great, the rest of the men joined them. They acted like kids on holiday, splashing one another and playing king of the mountain, with one man on the shoulders of another trying to dislodge the opponent. They lingered in the warm sea until the sun began to sink below the horizon.

The flight to Johnston Atoll had been relatively short, so a day of rest was not required before the next leg. The plane took off early the morning of May 10th for a nine hour and twenty minute flight to Kwajalein Atoll, part of the Marshall Island chain. Croze landed the plane in the late afternoon and taxied up to one of the two seaplane ramps. Ground crews attached wheels to the plane and pulled it up the ramp and onto the apron.

When the men got out of the plane, they saw signs of the intense five-day battle that had occurred on the island in January 1944. Heaps of twisted and scorched metal, the remains of buildings, lay scattered around the base. The sight was sobering. It left no doubt in their minds that they had entered the war zone. The Marshall Islands had been held by the Japanese since the end of the First World War, and Japan considered the island to be an important part of their outer perimeter of defenses. Ultimately, however, when Admiral Spruance led a large force of men and ships from Pearl Harbor on January 31st, landing on the island at two inlets, the Americans overwhelmed the much smaller and ill-prepared Japanese army. The casualty count made it clear that the infamous Japanese determination to fight to the death had prolonged the conflict. They lost all but 53 men of their original garrison of 3,500. U.S. troops achieved victory on February 3, 1944.

Since then the Seabees had been working to rebuild the facilities on the base. "But guess what, guys," said Ensign Wheeler. "The barracks aren't done yet. We're going to have to make like boy scouts here. See those tents over there. That's the visiting crew quarters. They do have wooden floors so the sand fleas won't get you."

The men swam for an hour and then headed for the outdoor showers. Standing on a wooden platform, they pulled a yard-long chain attached to a 55 gallon barrel mounted on a rack above the men's heads. Just enough fresh water trickled out to wet their bodies. They showered and returned to their tents. The evening's entertainment was a movie shown outdoors under the stars. They spent the following day swimming and tossing a coconut on the beach. With the Japanese long gone, the island was peaceful.

In the morning, they took off at 0800 for a nine hour flight to Saipan, located 120 miles north of Guam. The seaplane base was on the western side of the island, protected by a large reef that formed a lagoon stretching to white sandy beaches.

Croze put the plane down in the lagoon and taxied to the newly repaired seaplane ramp. The fuel barge met the plane, and the crew stayed aboard until the fueling was completed. After the ground crew attached the wheels and hauled the plane onto the apron, the men disembarked and stood gazing at the landscape. "It's incredible to think about how many people died here just last year," remarked Lyle Bumpas, as he looked around. "I remember the newsreels scared my folks since they knew that as a navy man I'd likely be coming out here."

"Well, it's quiet now. Let's go find our tents and stow our gear," said Garcia, hoping to break the mood. "Maybe we can try out that blue water pretty soon. I feel like I'm really needing that."

The sand ringing the deep blue of the lagoon gleamed in the sun. Waves gently slid onto the shore and receded with a soft hiss of bubbles. It was indeed a scene fit for a travel poster. Yet what the men had heard about the place was chilling. One of the fiercest battles in the Pacific had begun here on June 13, 1944. Fifteen American battleships and eleven cruisers opened up their guns, pounding the Japanese base for two days.

Then, on June 15th landing craft brought 8,000 marines ashore. They fought through tangles of barbed wire and took heavy fire from Japanese dug into machine gun emplacements and trenches. The Japanese were outnumbered. But, determined to fight to the last man, they staged the largest Bonzai attack in the war. Over 3,000 able-bodied men charged the American lines with orders to die for the Emperor. Behind the first wave, came the wounded, some bandaged, barely able to walk, and poorly armed.

Fueling the Plane at Saipan
(Compliments of National Archives)

When defeat proved inevitable, Emperor Hirohito sent a message urging the Japanese citizens on the island to commit suicide. Over 1,000 of them jumped over a cliff to their deaths. At the end of the battle, Vice Admiral Chuichi Nagumo, the naval commander who led the Japanese carriers at Pearl Harbor, committed suicide.

It was one of the costliest battles for the Americans in the Pacific War. Of the 71,000 men involved in the attack, the U.S. lost 2,949 killed and 10,464 wounded. Among the Americans wounded was Hollywood actor Lee Marvin, shot in the buttocks during the assault on Mount Tapochau.

After dinner that first evening, a barber from the base set up his equipment outside the tents and gave the men haircuts. When it was his turn, Lyle asked the barber about a rumor he'd heard. "Do you think it's true, like some folks are saying, that there are still some Japanese hidden out in those mountains over there? Kind of like the Sasquatch stories we hear back home."

"Yeah, some of the local people say they have seen them. The Japs still think they are going to win the war, even though most of them around here are dead," said the barber. "Kind of crazy."

The next morning the crew gathered at the plane and did a thorough scrubbing of the interior. They used water hoses to clean the outside of the plane. After lunch they returned to their tent and were talking about how to spend the rest of the day. In just a few minutes, the skipper and the two junior officers showed up barefoot and shirtless, wearing only gym shorts. Wheeler was carrying a football. "Okay, men," Croze announced, "we're going to challenge you to a little game of touch football on the beach. Since both Mr. Hicks and I played football in college, we're going to level the odds and take on any five guys you choose for your team. We'll meet you on the beach in ten minutes."

"Yes, sir, we'll be there. I hope you won't be too embarrassed when we beat you," Stephenson joked.

On the beach, the two junior officers, Hicks and Wheeler, marked off the goal lines with coconuts and drew the side lines with a stick. The teams played a rousing good game for over an hour, ending with a score of officers 21 and enlisted men 14.

After the game, all of the men charged into the water, laughing and splashing. Lou Wheeler swam out a ways from the others. He enjoyed just floating, eyes closed, drifting in the sea, feeling the cool lap of water. As navigator on their long flights, he had to be alert for hours in the throbbing roar of the prop plane, checking charts and instruments, making calculations. It was nice just being part of the ocean for a few minutes, feeling the nibbles of small fish on his leg. Then came a shout. "Shark!" He jerked awake, started paddling furiously through the water churned by his buddies. He nearly got kicked in the face by Garcia. They all staggered dripping, spitting, and breathing hard onto the sand and stared back at the water. "Where?!" "What the hell! I don't see nothing." "Hey, who yelled that?" Wheeler noticed a couple of the boys grinning. These guys are something else, thought Wheeler, as he shook his head to clear his ears and joined the bunch trudging back over the hot sand toward their tent. Shark - my ass. He smiled to himself.

That night they all watched "Guadalcanal Diary" on the outdoor screen and cheered for the marines who won the long battle after being beaten back by the Japanese.

The following morning, Monday, March 14th, the crew took off from Saipan and flew toward Jinamoc Island off the southern tip of Samar Province on the southeastern coast of the Philippine Islands. It was a long, ten hour flight. They had orders to report to Patrol Bombing Squadron 20, abbreviated as VPB-20. Until May 1, 1945, the squadron had been based at Jinamoc but was now on the USS Pokomoke moored off the island of Tawi Tawi.

Late in the afternoon, Croze set the plane down on Leyte Gulf and taxied to the ramp at the U.S. Navy Seaplane Base on Jinamoc. There were no battle scars on the landscape here, but the island's name revealed its role in the war zone. When the military took over the island in 1944, they stripped away its native name and replaced it with an acronym. No longer Salvacion, it was now Jinamoc: Joint Intelligence Naval Air and Military Operation Center. The name stuck. As they sat waiting for the ground crew, Croze told Wheeler about how the island lost its name, "Salvation." "A little ironic, don't you think?" Croze said.

They were just beginning to wonder what was taking so long for ground help to arrive, when they received an advisory from Ground Control that facilities for parking their plane on the ramp would not be available until noon the following day. Several planes had arrived that day and were expected to depart by mid-morning. Croze moored the plane to a buoy about fifty yards from the ramp and told the crew to stand down.

Wheeler and Huls took a small boat to the base and returned an hour later with box lunches and fresh fruit for the crew. "Hey, where's the beer, Mr. Wheeler?" Charlie Moorfield asked.

"Sorry, guys, you'll have to settle for cola and orange sodas. At least they're cold."

That night, the men sat around in the after-compartment talking about the war. It was hot and humid. Most of the guys had taken off their shirts and opened the side waist hatches in hopes of catching a little breeze. For security, no interior lights were on. The men were playing cards using a flashlight. Suddenly—panic! First a voice, then two Asian faces appeared outside the plane looking in at them. The crew scrambled to their feet and stumbled in all directions trying to find one of the rifles that were stowed in the compartment. "No Japanese! - no Japanese!" the Asians yelled. "We Filipinos…We friends!"

The men laughed, but their hearts were still pumping. They helped the Filipino soldiers into the plane. "We saw you land this afternoon," they explained. "We have souvenirs if you like to swap."

"So how'd you guys get out here?" Hicks asked.

"We swam - it's not far. When new guys come, they like souvenirs. We hold the bag out of the water - like this." He hefted a canvas bag above his head. They talked for an hour about the war and how bad it was for them when the Japanese occupied their country. Hicks traded a T-shirt for a small wooden bowl he thought his wife would like. Kenny bought a bracelet made of wooden beads for his sister. Several others

Fatal Error

exchanged some coins for a few trinkets. Just before midnight, the soldiers slipped into the water toting their canvas bag and swam back to their base.

Early the next morning, a small boat brought breakfast to the crew. Clearance to taxi to the ramp finally came at 2 pm. Once the plane was towed into a parking area near the repair depot, the men untied their sea bags from the upper bunks, opened the lower compartment door, and tossed them onto the ground. They were tired and hungry. It was a relief to know that this time they were on a substantial base. No platform tents here. When the navy built a seaplane base on Jinamoc, they brought in forty-five Quonset huts for berthing, with additional huts for a hospital, dining, and recreational facilities. The Seabees constructed fuel and repair depots and built a cement ramp on the ocean side of the island because the water there was deep enough for seaplane operations. Seabees graded taxiways and hard stands for the planes that were out of the water. Both PBY Catalinas and PBM Mariners flew anti-submarine and anti-shipping missions from Jinamoc.

After the officers departed, Crow and Garcia were the first two enlisted men off the plane. They picked up their seabags and tossed them onto their shoulders. "I don't know about you, Kenny, but I'm ready for a hot shower and a good meal," Garcia said.

"Boy, me too, Joe, let's find our building. Mr. Wheeler said it was number 29B." The two men walked past two buildings before they found the right one. A note on the entrance said bunks 18 through 26 were for their crew. The two men threw their seabags on their bunks, stripped off their clothes and headed for the shower, just as the rest of the crew began to arrive. They didn't need a map to find the chow hall - the strong aroma of roasting beef led the men to the right place, another Quonset hut. A sign said, "Take all you want but eat all you take." They would have no problem following that order. The men loaded their trays, got a slice of apple pie from the end of the table, and filled their glasses with milk. They sat at an empty table toward the back and ate in silence. They were too hungry for conversation.

That night they watched a movie at an indoor theater built into a large Quonset hut. Movietone News was first. Lowell Thomas announced that Mussolini had been captured and killed by Italian partisans. All the men in the theater cheered and whistled. But sobering news followed. Seventeen U.S. ships had been sunk by Japanese kamikaze attacks at Okinawa. "Oh my god, my brother Alva is in that battle of Okinawa," Charlie Moorfield whispered to Igoe who was sitting beside him. When the movie started most of the men forgot the war for an hour while they watched Walt Disney's "Dumbo." But Charlie sat slumped in his chair. He didn't find the antics of a flying elephant of much interest.

After the movie, Igoe pulled Moorfield aside as they walked out into the night air. "Don't worry, Charlie, didn't you tell me your brother was on a battleship?" said Igoe, trying to reassure him. "It would take a hundred kamikazes at once to even put a dent in a battleship."

"Thanks, John, I hope he's okay. He's my only brother. I've missed him a lot," Charlie said. "It has been tough for my parents, too, with both of us in the war. It was great we were able to spend leave-time at home together back in January." That night Charlie lay awake. He did not share Igoe's optimism regarding the safety of battleship crews.

On May 17th the crew departed Jinamoc Island for their final destination of Tawi-Tawi.

CHAPTER 6

Tawi-Tawi, Philippine Islands

May 17, 1945

AFTER THREE HOURS IN THE air, the crew was approaching their final destination of Tawi-Tawi. From the bow gun position, Joe Garcia could see a necklace of tree-filled islands, part of the Sulu Archipelago. Moments later he spotted the camouflaged hull of the seaplane tender USS Pokomoke, anchored a few thousand feet from a small island. A chill ran down his back and his pulse quickened. "Holy shit, we're here," he muttered. "All that training, those practice flights, the time we spent in Banana River, San Diego and Hawaii, and now we're here. They could be shooting at us by tomorrow. No, screw that," he thought, "we'll be shooting them down and sinking them. I can't believe we're finally in the war."

As the plane approached the landing area, the pilots could see several PBM-5 seaplanes tied to buoys located around the USS Pokomoke. A huge crane was hoisting one PBM-5 up the side of the ship.

Croze eased the Mariner down and made a graceful landing about a half mile from the ship. As he began to taxi toward the Pokomoke, a coxswain in an approaching small boat gestured for the plane to follow him. The boat led them to a buoy, and the men in the boat helped moor the

USS Pokomoke (AV-9)
(Compliments of National Archives)

PBM-5. After the plane was secured, Lyle Bumpas reached out through the bow hatch and helped three of the sailors from the boat climb into the aircraft.

"We're your plane guards," one of the men explained. "We'll keep a watch on the plane so all you guys can go to the ship. It's something we do for all the plane crews here."

When they arrived at the USS Pokomoke, they clambered up the ladder leading to the quarterdeck. Croze saluted the officer of the deck and requested permission to come aboard. "Permission granted, Lieutenant," said the officer, returning the salute. "Lieutenant Commander Harper is waiting for you on the after deck, sir. My messenger will show you and your crew the way."

About half way to the after deck, Croze saw Harper striding toward him. "Hey, DeLand, welcome aboard. I'm Bob Harper. Sorry I wasn't on the quarterdeck to meet you, but I've been tied up with a problem back here with one of our planes."

When the crew was assembled on the after deck, Harper formally welcomed them to Patrol Bombing Squadron 20. He and the operations officer, Lieutenant Walter "Skip" Forsha, shook hands with each member of the crew. "We're certainly glad to have you men here with us," Harper said. "It's noisy topside, and I know you have a lot to do to get settled on the ship. I've arranged a meeting with all of you and other members of our squadron at 0800 tomorrow morning in the squadron briefing room. Right now the messenger will give you a quick tour of the Pokomoke then take you men to your berthing compartment so you can stow your gear."

The messenger led the men through the ship, showing them the crew's mess, the laundry, the squadron office, and the crew's recreation room, equipped with a pool table and two ping pong tables. There were small tables and chairs for writing letters, several decks of cards, and a stack of old magazines.

When the men went back to the quarterdeck with plans to return to the plane for their seabags, they found them on the main deck, neatly stacked. "Look at this," Eddie Calhoun said. "I could get used to this kind of service real fast. First they guard our plane, then deliver our bags. It makes me feel important."

"You are important, Eddie." Owen Huls assured him. "Most of the guys from the Pokomoke don't risk their lives in enemy territory like we'll be doing real soon." The men grabbed their seabags and took them to the berthing compartment.

Skip Forsha showed the three officers to their rooms. Wheeler and Hicks shared a two-man stateroom with bunk beds and Croze had a private room. Forsha explained that the cots in each room were for sleeping topside if their state rooms were too hot. The enlisted men sleep on the after deck and the officers up forward.

At 0800 the next morning, the crew mustered in the squadron briefing room to meet with officers and senior enlisted members of the squadron. Lieutenant Skip Forsha briefed them on the current situation of the war of the Pacific. The battle of Okinawa that began on April 6th was still raging, he told them. The Japanese were so desperate they deployed a thousand kamikaze planes to crash into the U.S. Fleet with a huge loss of life and ships for the Americans.

Then Lieutenant Commander Harper spoke: "Good morning, men, I want to welcome you to Tawi-Tawi and to Patrol Bombing Squadron 20. The USS Pokomoke will be your home for the foreseeable future, and the ship's crew will do everything they can to make you as comfortable as possible." Charlie Moorfield sat staring at the floor. After the news about Okinawa, he was struggling to keep his focus on Harper's voice as he continued his formal speech: "With your arrival, we have 15 PBM-5 Mariner aircraft manned by 61 officers and 171 combat air crewmen. You are joining an exceptionally fine and dedicated group of men in this squadron. Tomorrow you will make your first war patrol. You'll have a senior pilot and three experienced crewmen with you to judge your level of readiness to patrol on your own. Good luck, gentlemen, I expect each one of you to do your very best to help our country and our allies win this war with Japan."

When the speech ended, Charlie watched as Harper called Croze aside for a moment and then left the room. Croze addressed the crew, assuring them of his confidence in their combat capability. He urged them to take the rest of the day to get settled on the ship and to be ready for an early departure in the morning. After dismissing the crew, he asked Ensign Wheeler and Charles Moorfield to remain.

"Moorfield, the ship's chaplain wants to talk to you. Mr. Wheeler will go with you. There is a messenger waiting outside who will take you to the chaplain's office."

"What's going on, sir? Why does he need to talk to me?"

"I'm sorry, Moorfield, I don't know. They told me to send you right away."

On the way to the chaplain's office, Moorfield looked at Wheeler with a strained expression. "What do you think this is about, Mr. Wheeler? I'm afraid it might be about my brother, Alva. Ever since we started getting reports on what's happening at Okinawa, I've been worried. He's a gunner on a battleship there."

"I don't know, but let's keep our fingers crossed and hope for the best."

The messenger escorted the two men to an office with a sign that read Ship's Chaplain. Moorfield knocked at the door, and a voice boomed, "The door is open."

"Will you come in with me, Mr. Wheeler? I don't feel very good about this."

"I'm right here with you, Charlie."

The two men entered the office. Behind a desk was a slender middle-aged man with dark receding hair and round wire-rimmed glasses, wearing the uniform of a lieutenant commander. He stood up to welcome them. "I'm Chaplain Cook," he said, as he shook hands with both men. "Are you Charles Moorfield?"

"Yes, Padre, I am," Moorfield responded, using the common title given to chaplains of all denominations.

"Charles, I'm very sorry to tell you your brother, Gunners Mate First Class Alva Moorfield, was killed on May 12th at Okinawa. A kamikaze made a direct strike on his ship, USS New Mexico, destroying the gun mount your brother was in charge of. He died instantly, Charles, he didn't suffer."

Moorfield closed his eyes and dropped his head for a moment. "I knew it, I knew it, son of a bi... sorry, Padre, I didn't mean to cuss, but when I saw the newsreel about the kamikaze attacks at Okinawa, I just had a terrible feeling." His lip began to quiver and his eyes filled with tears. He thought about his mother, how she had cried when he and his brother, Alva, returned to the navy after their January leave.

The chaplain put his hand on Moorfield's shoulder to comfort him.

"He was my only brother, Padre, what are my parents going to do? And I'm not home to help them through this."

'Your brother gave his life for our country. That's something we all must to be willing to do. God bless you, Charles, I'll pray for you and for your brother."

Wheeler walked back to the main deck with Moorfield. "I'm really sorry about your brother, Charlie. If there is anything I can do for you, don't hesitate to come and talk to me, okay?"

"Thanks, Mr. Wheeler, I appreciate it. Even though you're about the same age as the rest of the guys, we all look up to you as a big brother. You're always there for us."

Moorfield joined the rest of the crew and didn't say anything about his brother. He stayed busy and tried hard not to show any emotion or look the other men in the eyes. In the early evening, Dale Hunt came across Charlie lying on his bunk with his face toward the bulkhead rather than playing pool in the rec area with the rest of the men. "Hey, are you sick or something?" he asked. "You've been pretty quiet all day." Charlie finally confessed his loss. "But don't say anything, Dale, I don't want to talk about being killed in battle when we're about to make our first war patrol. The guys are nervous enough. The skipper and Mr. Wheeler are the only other ones who know about this."

At 0630 the following morning, May 23, 1945, the crew met in the squadron briefing room. Lieutenant Skip Forsha introduced Lieutenant Howard Rumrey, the pilot being relieved by Croze. He also introduced three inspectors who would fly along with the crew. Forsha explained they would be making an attack on enemy shipping near Sandakan Harbor, on the northern coast of Borneo, a distance of 140 miles from Tawi-Tawi.

By 0730 the plane was in the air flying southwest toward Sandakan Harbor. Del Croze was the pilot and Lieutenant Rumrey sat in the co-pilot seat. The inspectors were assigned to different areas of the plane to assess the crew's performance. "Good job, Del," Rumrey said. "You and your crew's pre-flight checks were done well and your takeoff was text book perfect."

"Thanks, Howard, we've been working hard as hell for the past six months to get it right. We'll be glad to take over here for you and your crew. After all the patrols you guys have made, you deserve a rest."

Fatal Error

The men were nervous, thinking that at any minute they could be attacked by the Japanese. After an hour of searching for enemy shipping, Joe Garcia spotted something. "Bow gunner to pilot, looks like a couple of small black boats just leaving the island below."

Croze and Rumrey trained their binoculars on the two motorboats leaving Nunuyan Darat Island at the mouth of Sandakan Harbor. "Pilot to crew, we're going down to make an attack on two small boats. It looks like there are about a dozen Jap soldiers in each boat. Heads up, let's knock these guys out on the first pass. These targets are too small for bombs, so I'm relying on you gunners."

Lieutenant Rumrey had made this kind of attack dozens of times and was calm, but Croze felt the palms of his hands getting wet and his heart start pounding as he dove the plane directly toward the motorboats. Joe Garcia at the bow gun and Kenny Crow at the deck gun opened fire at the same time. They were both nervous and excited and their first round kicked up water behind the targets. After taking a deep breath, they began firing again and got direct hits. Four Japanese soldiers plunged over the side just before the two boats exploded, sending up a huge plume of black smoke that enveloped the PBM-5. As Croze pulled out of the dive, breaking into the clear air, tail gunner Dale Hunt opened fire on the four men in the water.

"I got 'em! I got those sons a bitches," Hunt yelled into the intercom. "Take that you yellow bastards, that's for Charlie's brother."

Most of the crew had no idea what Hunt was talking about. Lou Wheeler looked over at Charlie Moorfield, and they nodded to each other with a slight smile. Daulton Stephenson noticed the exchange of glances between Wheeler and Moorfield. He knew Moorfield's brother had been in the heat of battle at Okinawa, but he decided not to say anything until Moorfield mentioned it first.

Dale Hunt had often thought about how it would feel to kill another man. He wondered if he would feel sad or guilty or if he would enjoy

47

taking out an enemy. He didn't think he would like it, but those people had killed his best friend's brother. He felt a sense of accomplishment. No guilt. He talked to himself, alone in the tail gun turret, to make sure what he felt was right. "I know those bastards would have done that to me if they could have. And those frigin' kamikazes, our poor guys don't stand a chance against them. Yeah, we've heard about how they treat our men when they're prisoners of war. Those guys got what they deserved."

The rest of the afternoon Croze assisted six PT boats, directing them from the air to make attacks on targets in Sandakan Harbor. Lieutenant Rumrey brought the two co-pilots, one at a time, into the cockpit so he could see them in action.

At 6 p.m. Croze landed at Tawi-Tawi. Two inspectors were in the bow of the plane to observe the crew as they approached the mooring buoy. As Croze slowed the plane, Lyle Bumpas leaned out of the forward hatch with a boathook and made a perfect grab on the buoy. They tied up the plane and returned to the Pokomoke in a waiting boat.

The crew gathered in the squadron briefing room to hear Lieutenant Howard Rumrey's report to the squadron commander: "Commander Harper," he said, "as the chief inspector for Lieutenant Croze and his crew, it is my pleasure to report that this crew performed in an exceptional manner in all areas. The attack on enemy boats was made with speed and precision and the handling of the plane was flawless. After consulting with my inspectors, it is my opinion that this crew is ready to perform whatever duties they may be given."

"Thanks, Howard," Harper said. "Del, I want to congratulate you and each one of your men. I don't recall a single new crew that got such positive comments from the inspectors. You have my approval to patrol in all areas.

"I'll give you your first assignment right now. After a day of rest tomorrow, you will go on your first patrol alone on Friday, May 25th. You'll be working with PT boats at Sandakan Harbor again. We've received reports that the Japs have a bomber at Sandakan that they fly every night at dusk.

It's a long cylindrical two engine dive bomber we call a Val, just like the ones the Japs used against us at Pearl Harbor. So far, our pilots have not found it, but we would really like to dispose of it. They keep it well hidden, but if you find it, be sure to destroy it."

CHAPTER 7

Attack on Sandakan Harbor

May 25, 1945

AT 0600 ON THE MORNING of May 25, 1945, the crew was in the briefing room waiting for the skipper to arrive. "This is it, you guys, our first patrol without babysitters," Stephenson said raising his eyebrows.

Before anyone had a chance to reply, Croze entered the room with the two junior officers. "Good morning, men. We're on our own today, and we're heading back to Sandakan Harbor to work with two PT boats. This is our first opportunity to show 'em what we've got without people looking over our shoulders. This is what we've been training for, and I know you guys will be great. Let's give 'em hell!"

The men went out to their assigned PBM-5 to begin the pre-flight checks. The ordinance men picked up ammunition left in the waist compartment by the USS Pokomoke crew. Kenny Crow walked to the deck-gun turret carrying his box of .50 caliber ammo belts without talking to anyone. He was confident in his skills as a gunner, but he felt nervous. That same feeling permeated most of the crew members—like the first day on a new job. In this case, a potentially lethal new job.

Croze taxied toward the east into the orange and yellow morning sky. After take-off, he turned and headed for Sandakan Harbor on the north coast of Borneo. Marshall Hicks sat next to him in the co-pilot seat. Lou

Wheeler, the navigator for the day, passed recommended course changes to the pilot to keep the plane on track toward the target.

At 0745, they rendezvoused with two PT boats near the entrance to Sandakan Harbor. Croze made radio contact with the boats and reported two Japanese transport ships Calhoun had picked up on radar a few minutes earlier. The ships were five miles to the north, heading toward Sandakan. Upon receiving this information, the PT boats powered north on separate courses 100 yards apart in order to attack the transports from both sides. Croze reached the target ships ahead of the boats. He put the PBM-5 into a dive. "Pilot to bow and deck gunners. Aim at the rudders. Let's slow them down for the PT guys."

Garcia and Crow acknowledged and opened fire. "Think we nailed them," yelled Crow as they watched the two ships veer off course unable to steer. When the PT boats pulled into range, their crews fired two well-placed torpedoes that finished off the ships. As Croze dove again to take a look at the sinking ships, Garcia held up two fingers in a victory sign to the PT crew. They raised their hands with a thumbs-up cheer for Croze and his men.

"Pilot to crew, heads up, men. We are not done yet. We're going into the harbor to look for Jap ships. I expect we'll take some fire, so stay alert." Arriving over Sandakan Harbor, Croze announced, "Good pickings down there, men. Let's go get them." As Croze circled and dove again and again into the harbor, the gunners strafed and blasted Japanese cargo ships. They counted the wreckage as they pulled away: four ships sunk, three damaged. They then began a search of the area for the Japanese bomber reported to fly every evening at dusk. "Pilot to all stations, keep a sharp eye out for the Val bomber that Commander Harper said the Japs keep under wraps around here. I want to find that plane and keep it from ever flying again."

After an hour of searching, Garcia caught the gleam of metal winking through the heavy foliage of a large tree. "Bow gun to pilot, there is something pretty big behind that huge tree near the orange building."

"Good eyes, Garcia. I'll circle back for a determination. If it's a plane, I want you to give it everything you've got, understand? Aim at the wings."

Croze circled around and started a steep dive toward the tree and the building. "Got it-one Val dead ahead," he shouted. Garcia's pulse started racing as he fired with both guns, aiming at the engine and right wing. The wing collapsed just as Croze released a 250 pound bomb. The plane blew apart in an immense fire ball, hurling shrapnel in all directions. Garcia let out a deep breath and wiped the sweat from his forehead with his sleeve.

"Pilot to crew, it's still early and we are out of bombs. We are returning to Tawi-Tawi to re-arm. They may send us back here. Looks like there are still targets down there in the harbor."

Croze contacted the squadron and requested a bomb crew be available to load additional 250 and 500 pound bombs and a fuel barge to top off the fuel tanks. He reported an ETA of 1300 hours and began their hour-long flight back to the base.

At Tawi Tawi as they waited on the moored plane for the bombs to be loaded and the fuel tanks topped off, Croze turned to Hicks. "Take over here, Marshall, I want to go forward for a minute and talk to Garcia." Croze stuck his head into the bow gun turret. "Great job with that Jap plane, Garcia, your aim was perfect. The squadron will be very happy to know we destroyed it." He reached in and shook Garcia's hand and started back toward the cockpit. Jeez that kid can shoot, he thought. I never figured that little guy would turn out to be such a hot gunner.

At 1430 hours the crew took off again. With a change in orders from the squadron, they set a course for Darvel Bay, 109 miles south-south-west from Tawi-Tawi. Their targets were Japanese-occupied structures. Over the town of Semporna, Croze dropped two 500 pound bombs, destroying two buildings occupied by Japanese soldiers, despite heavy fire from anti-aircraft guns. Swerving away from the flak, Croze turned south toward the town of Mostyn where they bombed three more enemy-occupied buildings. The crew returned to Tawi-Tawi at dusk, exhausted but happy with their successful day.

After a day of rest, the crew was told to prepare for a return to Sandakan Harbor, this time as part of a major assault team led by Lieutenant Richard Monahon's squadron of nine PT boats. Australian fighter planes were joining them to provide air cover while the slower, heavier PBM-5 Mariners were strafing and bombing targets in the harbor. Assisting in the attack was the squadron commander, Lieutenant Commander Bob Harper, piloting a second Mariner. He was impressed by Croze and his crew and wanted to see them in action. The two PBM-5s took off from Tawi-Tawi at 0530 on the morning of May 27, 1945.

Daylight was just breaking as the nine PT boats raced into the harbor at 35 knots spewing a heavy layer of smoke for protection against the enemy. They fired torpedoes at several enemy installations, shattering docks and attached buildings. The radio crackled as Lieutenant Monahon called the Mariners for support. "Mariner Leader, this is PT leader, over."

"PT Leader, go ahead, this is Mariner leader," Harper responded.

"We are getting a lot of flak from three gunnery installations about 1000 yards inside the harbor on the west side. We have targets we want to hit in that area, but the big guns are keeping us at bay. Do you think you can take care of them for us?"

"Roger, that. We'll quiet them for you."

"Harper to Croze, follow me, we're descending for an attack on those three large gun emplacements on the west bank."

"Roger, I'm right behind you."

Croze addressed his crew. "Pilot to gunners, get ready to give those targets all the lead you can pump out." Once again Croze's gunners were put to the test. Garcia and Crow blasted the gun emplacements getting direct hits. Both Mariners dropped bombs that destroyed two of the guns. They left the third inoperable.

"Mariner leader, this is PT leader. Great job, you guys, I'm impressed."

The two PBM-5 Mariners then came around for an attack on three Japanese transport ships, severely damaging both. They dropped instantaneous fused depth charges on two barracks, blowing them apart and leaving them in flames. The pilots carefully avoided a prisoner of war camp located on the outskirts of Sandakan. The PT boats, meanwhile, continued to destroy everything they could in the harbor, including a cluster of Japanese suicide boats that were nearing completion at the local saw mill.

With all targets eliminated, both Mariners returned to Tawi-Tawi. They landed on parallel courses. Croze slowed to allow the squadron commander to tie up his plane first. When they were moored, the men went to the briefing room on the USS Pokomoke. Lieutenant Commander Harper addressed the crew: "Congratulations, men," he said, "you have just participated with great success in the largest attack on Sandakan so far in this war. I am assured you are now ready for your first twelve-hour patrol. You can take a week to prepare. Study charts of the regions of Borneo, Balikpapan, the Strait of Makassar, and the Celebes and take a good look at photos of the types of ships you may find. I'll be discussing your route with your skipper and navigators. Once again, good work today."

The officers headed for the ward room, and the men went to the crew's mess hall for a well deserved meal. "Check this out, Irish, we're having corned beef and cabbage," Garcia said as he poked Igoe in the ribs with his elbow.

"Well, it's not like me Mum used to make, but it beats hot dogs," Igoe said, giving his usual response to the navy's corned beef.

After dinner the men watched a movie and later decided to sleep topside. Garcia and Igoe set up their cots side by side on the after deck.

"Good night, mate. I hope you have a good sleep. Be sure to dream about Texas."

"Yeah, you too, Irish, I'll see you in the morning. You can dream about Texas, too, if you want, you'd love it there. You should come and visit me in Corpus Christi after the war."

"That would be great. We can go hunting and fishing together. I think I'll dream about that. G'night."

The crew's happy dreams that night were possible only because they did not know the horrific consequences of their day of victory. A group of twenty-five Japanese Marines, dedicated to die for the Emperor, had arrived in Sandakan to man the suicide boats being built there. When the Americans destroyed every one of the boats in the attack, the Marines were infuriated. The loss terminated their dreams of glory as war heroes. They went berserk, running through the city, killing every local citizen they could find. Meanwhile, the Japanese military, angered by an almost complete destruction of their harbor facilities, rounded up all English-speaking people, herded them to a cemetery, and beheaded them. They ultimately burned the entire city, including the prisoner of war camp that housed Australian and British prisoners, forcing the prisoners on a death march from Sandakan to Ranau, 160 miles southwest.

CHAPTER 8

First Long War Patrol

June 4, 1945

JOE GARCIA LOOKED UP AT the stars from his old army cot on the after deck of the USS Pocomoke. He knew it was time to get up, but he wanted a few more minutes to think about home. He was apprehensive about the day's long war patrol and didn't want to think about it this early. Corpus Christi, Texas, seemed a million miles away from the ship, anchored on the southern tip of the Philippines. It seemed like just yesterday he said goodbye to his family and his girlfriend, Mary. Joe closed his eyes. He could see Mary's face just as clearly as if she were there with him. A sudden cold chill ran down his back, but he shrugged it off and focused again on Mary's face.

"I love you Joe, I'll be right here waiting for you when you come home after the war. It can be four years, Joe, I'll still be here."

The splashing of a school of fish fleeing a predator brought Joe back to reality. When he opened his eyes, a little sliver of moon gave just enough light so he could see a faint outline of their PBM-5, moored to a buoy fifty yards off the port bow of the ship. He looked around the deck and saw cots everywhere with sleeping sailors. A few of them were covered with a sheet, but like Joe, most were sleeping in just their white navy issue boxer shorts with no cover at all. They were near the equator where the summer sun heated the ship like a blowtorch. It was almost impossible to sleep in the berthing compartment below decks. At least topside they could get an occasional morning breeze. He knew he had to get up soon. It was June 4, 1945, and they had a 0600 lift off time for their first 12 hour war patrol.

Garcia had developed into a tough combat air crewman, but physically he was small. When he joined the navy he was just five feet two inches tall and weighed 123 pounds. He usually did not let his small size bother him. He was smart, confident, good looking and a good athlete. All the girls flirted with him and that was good enough for him. But if someone tried to make something of it, teasing him for being a shrimp, he used the skills he had learned as a champion boxer to put the bully in his place.

Garcia glanced at his watch. It was 0415 and time to get up. He needed to shower, shave, and get dressed before morning chow at 0500. He looked over at the cot next to him where John Igoe was still snoring lightly. Joe yawned and stretched then tapped Igoe on the shoulder. "Hey, Irish, wake up, it's 0415."

John Igoe always set his cot up next to Garcia's. At just eighteen years old, Garcia was the youngest member of their seaplane crew. Igoe was thirty-six and the oldest member of the crew. Sleeping next to Garcia made him feel like a father looking after the son he never had. Igoe was born in Ireland and immigrated to the US when he was 19 years old. He lived with his sister Mary, her husband, and their three daughters. When his sister's husband died suddenly at the age of 35, John helped her raise the three girls, giving up the chance to get married and have his own family. The men in the crew became his family.

"Okay, Joe Harvey, I'm getting up," Igoe said in his soft Irish accent. He knew Garcia's family and close friends called him Joe Harvey, so he picked up the habit of calling him that as well.

Joe Harvey Garcia
(Compliments of Richard Garcia)

The two men stowed their cots, showered, and headed for breakfast.

John Igoe looked around the dining room and mentally counted all the crew members. As the senior enlisted member of the crew, he took his responsibilities seriously. The skipper had told him they would be taking two riders along with them today, and he made sure they were eating with the crew. When the men were seated, Igoe walked over to the riders to introduce himself.

"Welcome aboard, men, I'm John Igoe, the crew chief."

Both riders, meteorologist Donald Pell and machinist's mate Robert Jezewski, introduced themselves.

"Where are you blokes from?" Igoe asked. "Any special reason you're riding with us today?"

"I'm from Brazil, Indiana," Pell replied, "and I'm a meteorologist. I brief all the pilots on weather conditions before each patrol, so I'll be taking weather observations along the route."

Robert Jezewski said he had lived in Milwaukee all his life until he joined the navy. "I repair those big engines on the PBM-5s. All of us that work on the engines have to ride on the planes. I think they just want to make sure we do a good job," Jezewski said with a smile.

"Welcome," Igoe said, "we're glad to have you aboard."

When the crew members had finished breakfast, they stowed their personal items and prepared to head out to the plane. The three aviation machinist's mates took the first boat, since it was their responsibility to make sure every system on the plane was in proper working order. As soon as they were aboard, John Igoe, Daulton Stephenson, and Lyle Bumpas started making their pre-flight checks. From under the flight engineer position, Igoe yelled, "Hey, Stephy, we got a small leak in one of the hydraulic lines. You got a roll of cloth tape somewhere?"

"Think that'll do it?"

"Yeah, should hold till the repair shop gets down here after our run. Hell, with the parts shortage we've got around here, tape and baling wire's about all that's keeping these birds in the air. I think this damn thing was leaking last time we had her out."

John Patrick Igoe
(Compliments of Jim Carter)

The four ordnance men - Dale Hunt, Kenny Crow, Charlie Moorfield and Joe Garcia - took the second boat to the plane. They carried seven M1 rifles and three .38 caliber Smith and Wesson pistols that they would use only in a rare hand to hand combat situation. The night before, the bomb crew from the USS Pokomoke dropped off five boxes of .50 caliber ammunition belts in the waist compartment of the PBM-5. They also loaded three 500-pound bombs and six 250-pound bombs into the bomb bays in the rear of the engine compartments. The men in the bomb crew took delight in writing their personal messages on each of the bombs. "Up yours, Tojo" and "Remember Pearl Harbor" were some of their favorite messages. The ordnance men grabbed several ammunition belts from the boxes and went to load and check their guns.

Joe Garcia squeezed himself into the bubble in the nose of the plane to load and check his guns. His small frame was a perfect fit for that cramped space. After loading the guns, he gently rubbed his hands along the portion of the barrels that were inside the plane. He talked to the guns as if they were alive. "We're going to give it to 'em today, huh, guys, just like we did on our first three patrols. We're going to blast those Jap bastards right out of the ocean." He loved being in the nose turret with nothing between him and the enemy but a thin piece of plastic. As the bow gunner, Joe imagined he was flying the plane himself when they dove to strafe enemy targets.

The two radiomen, Owen Huls and Eddie Calhoun, picked up the food the cooks had prepared for the crew. Just before takeoff, Lieutenant Croze requested a boat to take him, the two junior officers, the radiomen, plus the two riders to the plane. As soon as he got aboard, the skipper met with the crew in the waist compartment for a pre-flight briefing. John Igoe made his report. "All systems checked and operating properly sir, the plane is ready for takeoff."

Del Croze acknowledged and addressed the crew. "Good morning, men. Today will be our first twelve-hour patrol. On our previous three missions we had shorter runs to assigned target areas. This time we will be on a scouting mission. The Seventh Fleet Air Command has ordered us to scour the east coast of Borneo as far as

Donald Milton Pell
(Compliments of Patricia Pell)

the northern edge of Balikpapan where the Japs have a huge oil supply. That target is heavily fortified and is being handled by the heavy bombers. When we reach Balikpapan, we'll turn and head across the Strait of Makassar to the west coast of the Celebes *(now known as Sulawesi, Indonesia)*, looking for enemy ships that are supplying the Japs on Borneo. We'll follow the Celebes coastline to the north then head home."

Croze looked around the room and noticed a nervous stare on the faces of several crew members. He asked if there were any questions and with no response, he continued. "Except for local fishing boats, anything that moves in the water is fair game. Combat Information has advised that a Jap gunboat has been operating in the south end of our patrol area. So far the pilots in our squadron haven't seen it, but I plan to find it today. I expect each one of you to be vigilant. When we find that gunboat, I'll need the help of every one of you to destroy it."

"Yes, sir," Kenny Crow said. "We'll blow all them bastards out of the water, Mr. Croze."

Croze smiled at Kenny's comment as he and Wheeler headed for the cockpit to make their pre-flight checks. Marshall Hicks pulled out the updated charts he had just gotten from the squadron and started to plot their course.

"Can I give you a hand plotting the course, Mr. Hicks?" Daulton Stephenson asked. He loved navigation and often helped the navigator with his job.

"Sure, Stephy. Start plotting with these new charts, and I'll get the camera ready so we can show the world how we are winning this war. Just remind me later, I'll give you copies of some of the photos."

"Thanks, Mr. Hicks, maybe I can show them to my grand kids some day," Stephenson said with a wink.

"Sure hope that's the case, Stephy."

Outside the plane, Lyle Bumpas inspected the plane's exterior from a station boat while the pilots cycled the ailerons, flaps, and rudder. Before he got back into the plane, Bumpas released the plane from the buoy and let it drift free.

Owen Huls sat at the radio operator's station directly behind the co-pilot. He tuned the transmitter and receiver to the ground control frequency and listened to make sure no one was transmitting. The only thing he heard was a faint crackle of static and a distant voice in a language he didn't recognize. Huls picked up the microphone, held it for a few seconds, and then pressed the transmit button. "Pokomoke, this is Mariner 062, radio check, over."

"Mariner 062, this is Pokomoke, read you loud and clear, out."

The junior radioman, Eddie Calhoun, sat at the radar station across from Huls. The radar had already been turned on during the pre-flight checks, so he just sat there watching Hulls make the radio check with the Pokomoke. I'd rather be in his chair, he thought. I didn't become a radioman just to sit here watching this little green screen.

John Igoe took his seat at the flight engineer's station. He checked the fuel level in each tank and scanned the instrument panel for proper power levels in all areas of the plane. In the cockpit, Croze and Wheeler had completed their pre-flight checks. They tested each of the engines one by one. When the engines were revved to maximum RPM, the noise was deafening, and the plane rocked from side to side. Once the tests were completed, Croze looked over at Wheeler. "You ready to take on some Jap war ships, Lou?"

"I'm ready," Wheeler responded. He kept his words short and crisp, so he wouldn't give away the nervousness he felt. "Want me to radio for permission to take off, sir?"

'I'll do it, Lou," Croze said, as he reached for the microphone. "Ground Control, this is Mariner 062, we are ready for takeoff, request clearance."

"Mariner 062, this is Ground Control. You are cleared for takeoff. Proceed on course 090 degrees."

The plane vibrated as both Croze and Wheeler eased the throttle control levers forward. Croze swung the plane around to 090 degrees and then shoved the throttles to maximum. The plane bucked, shuddered, and then surged forward, bouncing through the water. Both pilots kept a tight grip on the throttles as they glanced back and forth between the water ahead of them and their air speed indicator. "Now!" yelled Croze. Lou Wheeler activated the Jet Assisted Takeoff Pods. With one final bounce, the Mariner shot up out of the water. The two pilots gave each other a brief glance and a nod. They were airborne.

PMB-5 Jet Assisted Takeoff
(Photo from National Archives)

Croze kept a steady course and climbed to an altitude of 500 feet. He circled around and headed back over the USS Pocomoke to test the Identification Friend or Foe system. He then set a course for Borneo.

Daulton Stephenson had just completed plotting the course for the day's patrol and was hunched over the navigator's desk leaning on his elbows. He looked around at the nearby crew members. Something felt wrong. He had a queasy feeling in his stomach about today's flight. Tapping his breast pocket to make sure he had his New Testament, he realized he had left it in his locker on the ship. He bowed his head for a short prayer. They were on their way.

CHAPTER 9

Along the East Coast of Borneo

June 4, 1945

DEL CROZE MAINTAINED A SOUTHERLY course at an altitude of 3,000 feet until they reached the east coast of Borneo and then dropped to 500 feet to search for any Japanese ships in the area. By this date, the war was winding down, and the Japanese had recalled many of their armed forces to guard Japan from what they believed was an inevitable ground attack by US and Allied forces. The Japanese still maintained strong defenses at Balikpapan to protect the oil fields and refineries they needed to continue the war effort.

After four and a half hours of searching without finding a single Japanese ship, Croze saw the first puff of black smoke a thousand feet ahead of them as they approached Balikpapan. Undoubtedly this was the heavily fortified Japanese oil storage facility he had been told to avoid. A warning shot from the Japanese was all he needed to make a quick dogleg turn to the east and follow his assigned route across the Makassar Strait toward the Celebes.

Eddie Calhoun had been sitting at the radar screen all day without seeing a single contact. Suddenly, three blips appeared. "Radar to Pilot, three bogies dead ahead, sir, ten thousand yards."

"Pilot to Radar, good job, Calhoun, those targets should be right ahead of us. Keep an eye on them."

Within a few minutes the targets came into view. "There they are, skipper - looks like two Japanese merchants with a gunboat escort," said Wheeler. "Probably that PC-4 is the gunboat the squadron warned us about."

"You're right, Lou, and those merchants are loaded with supplies for the Japs at Balikpapan. We need to take them out first."

"Pilot to Crew, stand by for an attack on three Japanese ships. We have a couple of merchants with a military escort. We're going to take some fire, so be ready."

From the bow gun turret, Joe Garcia studied the ships. He felt adrenalin rushing through his body and his heart was pounding. He wiped his hands on his trousers and grabbed the twin .50 caliber guns.

Croze made a steep dive and lined up on the outboard cargo ship. Garcia and Crow started blasting from the bow and deck guns at the same time. They could see Japanese sailors running on the deck of their ship looking for cover. Three men jumped over the side to avoid the shells. Just as they reached the first ship, Croze released a 250 pound bomb. It arced through the air and hit the ship, blowing it apart.

They circled around and began an attack on the second ship. By this time the gunboat had manned their antiaircraft guns and had begun firing shells at the plane, but Croze held his course. Once again the bow and deck guns of the PBM-5 blasted the ship, and their second bomb skimmed down the side of the ship, detonating at the water line. The side of the ship blew apart as it rolled over on its side and began to sink.

Shells from the gunboat were exploding near the plane, filling the sky with puffs of smoke. Some of the explosions were close enough to rock the plane from side to side. Chunks of metal were bouncing off of the windshield and sides of the plane. Yet, once again Croze lined up for an attack. "Pilot to crew, we took out the two merchants, and we're going back to finish off the gunboat."

Just as they began their dive, there was a brilliant flash. A huge explosion shook the plane. Shrapnel crashed against the windshield. "We've been hit," Wheeler yelled as the plane rolled over on a 45 degree angle. Stunned for a moment, Wheeler shook his head and then grabbed the controls to help Croze stabilize the plane. Fuel oil from the wing tank was streaming down the side of the aircraft.

Moments later a second explosion rocked the plane in the opposite direction as a shell, penetrating the bottom of the plane, exploded in the crew's berthing compartment, ruptured one of the major fuel tanks, and blew a large hole in the bottom of the plane.

Croze and Wheeler were struggling to take evasive action just as a third shell detonated in the large waist compartment. The rear of the plane rose up, driving them into a steep dive. With the ocean rushing at them, Croze and Wheeler finally managed to pull the plane up and skimmed 50 feet above the water. They slowly gained altitude. Flight engineer, John Igoe, stared helplessly at the flight panel, blinking with warning lights.

Aft in the plane, Robert Jezewski, one of the riders from the USS Pokomoke, was writhing on the deck, screaming in pain. The final explosion had blown off his right foot. Donald Pell, who had been standing next to Jezewski was unhurt. He ripped off his belt and wrapped it around Jezewski's leg in an attempt to slow the blood flow. Nearby, Lyle Bumpas, struck in the back of the legs by red-hot lead, lay sprawled on the deck.

Marshall Hicks had been standing at the open waist compartment hatch taking pictures of the attack on the ships. The concussion blew him out of the plane. "Oh my god, Mister Hicks!" Charlie Moorfield yelled, still flat on his back from the explosion. Kenny Crow jumped down from the deck gun position and helped Moorfield to his feet. They went to the open hatch and saw Hicks dangling from his safety strap, banging against the side of the plane. "Hang on, sir, we'll pull you back in," Moorfield yelled, as he and Crow managed to find the strength necessary to drag Hicks up to the edge of the hatch. Hicks threw one leg inside, and the two men hauled him into the plane.

Three Hits on the Plane by the Japanese Gunboat
(Photo by the author)

"Thanks, guys," Hicks panted as he sat down and tried to catch his breath.

"We thought you took a dive without a parachute, Mr. Hicks. Good thing you had on that safety strap," Crow said.

"Oh, man, I can't believe what happened. I thought I was a gonner. You guys saved my life," Hicks said, as he looked at his hand that still had a tight grip on the camera. His head was spinning, and his heart felt like it was going to jump out of his chest.

Lyle Bumpas, who was lying on his belly, noticed there was a fire in the hydraulic lines. Although he was wounded and in pain, he pulled himself up and grabbed a fire extinguisher. Before he could get the fire under control, scalding hot hydraulic oil splashed on his leg and foot searing him with third degree burns.

"Lyle, your pants are smoldering," Moorfield yelled. He unzipped Bumpas's trousers and ripped them off, stomping on the burning pant leg. "Waist Gunner to Radio, we need the first aid kit back here right away."

Owen Huls grabbed the kit and ran aft to help the injured men. He first went to help Robert Jezewski, but when he saw his foot, he knew there was little he could do. He took a morphine styrette from the first aid kit and injected it into Jezewski's uninjured leg. Huls then turned his attention to Lyle Bumpas. "Try to stand still for a minute, Lyle, I need to bandage both of your legs," Huls said, struggling to keep Bumpas still. He bandaged both lower legs and then took the scissors, cut off the burned portion of Bumpas's trousers, and helped him put them back on.

Grimacing with pain, Bumpass still managed to say, "Thanks, Owen, I'm sure glad you took that First Aid class."

"Don't mention it, Lyle, you may have to help me some day."

Croze and Wheeler watched their controls closely as they fought to gain altitude, afraid that the yawing and pitching Mariner might stall if they pulled the nose up too fast. Finally they reached an altitude of 500 feet and leveled off. Yet the plane was still unstable, requiring both pilots at the controls to maintain lateral balance. In spite of their difficulty controlling the plane, the pilots set a course to return to Tawi-Tawi.

Croze put in a call, "Pilot to Flight Engineer. Igoe, what's going on? We're having a hell of a time keeping this thing level."

John Igoe responded with the bad news that they had lost two major fuel tanks. "I'm trying to pump fuel from the port wing tank to reposition the center of gravity and stabilize the plane."

"How much fuel have we got?"

"Two hours at max, sir."

"Roger that."

Croze thought about his options. The thought of not making it back to their base hadn't occurred to him, and he knew that putting the badly damaged plane down in open ocean could be catastrophic.

"Pilot to Navigator, give me the ETA to the Celebes coast line."

Stephenson, alone at the navigator desk, nervously shuffled the charts as he worked on an ETA. "Navigator to Pilot, this is Stephenson. I estimate it's about two hours."

"Stephenson, where is Mister Hicks?"

"He was aft in the plane with the camera when we got hit. I haven't seen him since."

"Go see if you can find him. It's going to be critical to get our coordinates out to the squadron. Since Mister Hicks has the most familiarity with the charts, we need him on the job."

Croze was concerned. He had forgotten that he gave Hicks permission to photograph the attack on the Japanese ships. If he was a casualty, they could be in trouble. Stephenson was still inexperienced. Croze felt some relief when Marshall Hicks reported in a few minutes later, saying that he was back at the navigation desk. But he could hear the strain in the Ensign's voice.

"Are you all right, Marshall?"

"Just shaken up, sir, it's pretty bad back there. But I'm okay. Stephenson and I are getting on top of things here."

"Good to hear. What's going on back aft?"

Hicks reported the damage to the compartment, the fire in the hydraulic lines, and the serious injuries to Jezewski and Bumpas. He didn't mention his narrow escape from death when he was blown out of the plane.

With the plane leveled on a course, Croze put through a radio call to the Pokomoke. "Flight Control, this is Mariner 062, over." Squadron Commander, Bob Harper, who was standing by in the flight control center, responded. "Go ahead, Del, I'm still here. What the hell is going on? We lost contact right after you notified us you were initiating another attack."

"We sank the two sugar dogs but got hit by the escort. Three direct hits, and we've lost two of our major fuel tanks. I think we can make it to the west coast of the Celebes by 1800 hours. We have a wounded man, a rider from Pokomoke, who needs medical attention and a crew member with shrapnel wounds and burns. We had a fire in the hydraulic lines.

"Okay, Dell, when you approach the Celebes, send me your latitude and longitude. Do that when you're still at altitude so we don't lose communication with you. We have a plane in the air, and I'll dispatch another from here. Stay at sea and keep your guns manned. We'll get to you just as quick as we can."

Croze acknowledged the orders from the squadron commander.

Two hours later the coastline of the Celebes came into view. "Pilot to Navigator, prepare our latitude and longitude and have the radiomen send it to the squadron just as soon as you get it done. I want it sent by Morse code so the squadron has a written copy of what we send."

The navigator delivered the latitude and longitude to the radiomen. Owen Huls contacted the squadron and sent the coordinates of their location.

Croze landed in the water, a mile from the coast line. As soon as the engines were shut down, he walked aft for a damage assessment. The plane reeked of smoke from the anti-aircraft explosions. He was stunned when he saw Robert Jezewski lying half conscious in a pool of blood. He knelt next to Jezewski to get a better look at his leg while Donald Pell explained what he had done to stem the flow of blood. "This is much worse than I thought. This man needs medical attention right away or he's not going to make it," Croze said.

Just then Igoe and Stephenson entered the waist compartment. "Skipper, we are taking on water from the huge hole blown in the hull. I don't know how much longer we can stay afloat. Should we start getting the men into the rubber life rafts?" Igoe asked.

Croze thought for a moment. "No, I'm going to taxi to shore and find medical attention for this man. He won't make it if we wait for the rescue planes." Croze restarted the engines. While still in deep water, he ordered the crew to destroy all classified material. They also jettisoned all equipment except for a radio transmitter and receiver.

By the time Croze and Wheeler taxied the plane onto the beach near the village of Lalombi, twenty miles south of the town of Donggala, it was 7 pm. The crew went ashore. John Igoe carried Robert Jezewski from the plane and eased him onto a stretcher that Eddie Calhoun brought to him. After scanning the area for a safe location, they chose a spot protected by large palms about 100 yards from the plane. Calhoun made a bed of dry straw and fashioned a canopy from a parachute to protect Robert from insects. He wrapped his foot in the cloth of a parachute to slow the bleeding and gave him another shot of morphine from their medical kit. He became mercifully unconscious.

John Igoe knelt down and made the sign of the cross. He reached under the parachute, put his hands on Jezewski's chest, and said a silent prayer. He then recited the Act of Contrition prayer out loud on behalf the unconscious man. Igoe looked at Robert's face and whispered, "May God be with you, my young friend, and may He hold you in the palm of His hand."

Lyle Bumpas was in pain but had managed to walk off the plane by putting his arm around Stephenson's shoulder. He had shrapnel wounds on both calves and third degree burns on his legs and feet. He picked two pieces of steel shrapnel from his left calf, but there were still imbedded pieces he couldn't reach.

When the crew got settled ashore, two curious natives who had seen the beached plane came by to find out what was going on. Lou Wheeler tried using sign language to tell them that they needed medical help for the wounded man. When he showed them Jezewski's foot, the natives nodded that they understood and ran off at full speed. Unfortunately, as the crew was soon to realize, they were running not to find a doctor but to alert the Japanese garrison at Donggala.

Del Croze gathered the men together. "I know you are all very concerned about the loss of our plane and being stuck on this island. We sent our location to the squadron, and they know where we are. Help will be here very soon. We can expect to see a rescue plane overhead within a few hours or no later than first light tomorrow morning. My biggest concern right now is the condition of our injured rider, Jezewski. Those native men that came by a few minutes ago have gone to get a doctor. Stay alert, I don't think there are any Japs in this area, but those two native men were able to walk in and surprise us. I don't want that to happen again. Keep a sharp look out for intruders and keep some flares ready to alert our rescue plane."

The ordnance men had carried rifles and pistols ashore with them along with all the small arms ammunition they had on the plane. Croze assigned four men to stand guard with rifles. He advised the rest of the crew to try to get some sleep.

Croze did not realize the Pokomoke's rescue team had an inaccurate report of their position. It read "QAL (*I am landing at*) SEA 00.00 degrees 119.20 E." The coordinates placed them on the equator at 00.00 degrees.

Equator

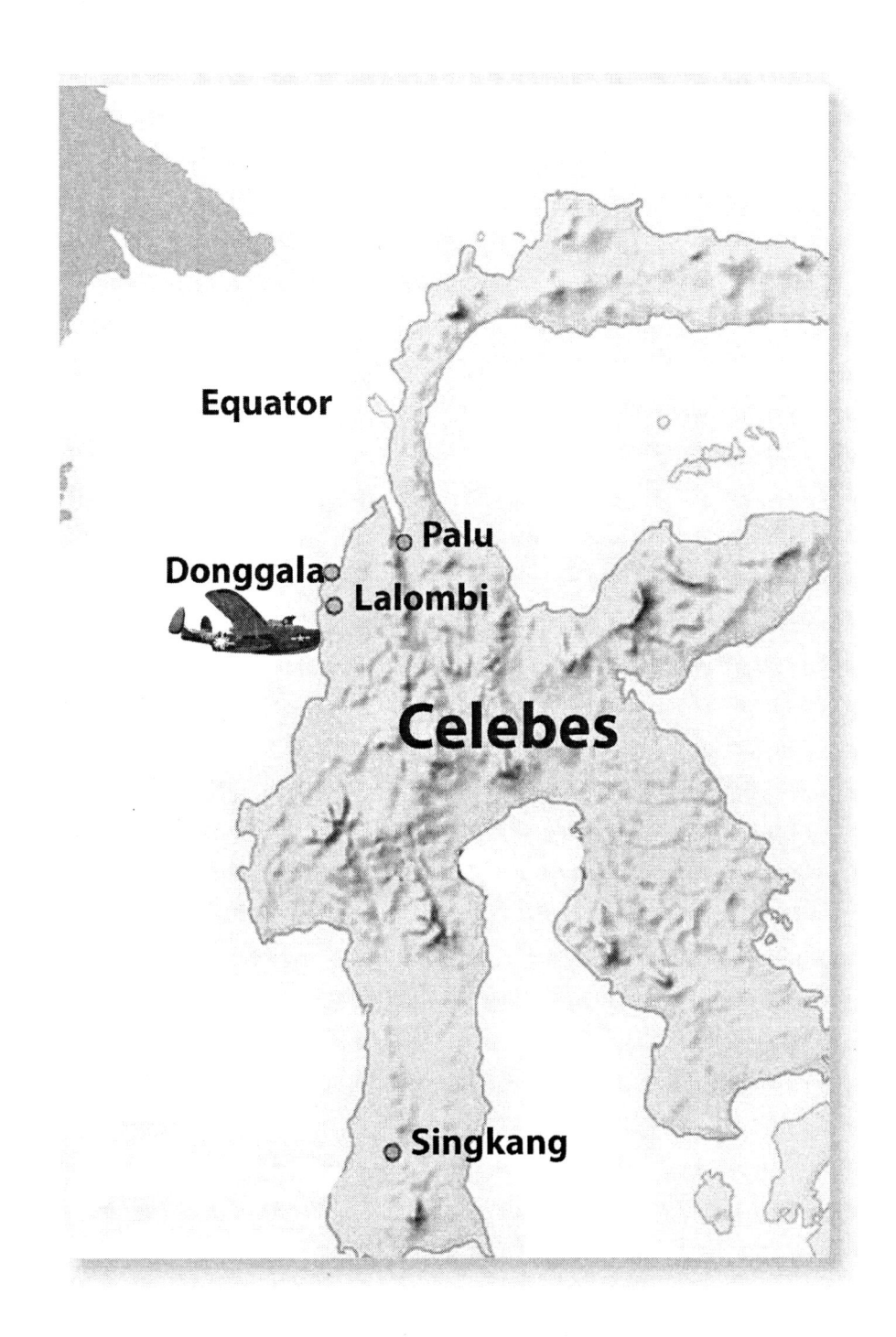

Donggala
Palu
Lalombi

Celebes

Singkang

However, their actual position was 00.50 degrees south, about 40 miles further south than their reported position. It is not known if the navigator who provided the coordinates, the radioman who transmitted the message, or the radioman who received the message made the mistake. Sadly, that one wrong number would prove to be a fatal error.

CHAPTER 10

Near Lalombi, Celebes, Dutch East Indies

June 5, 1945

Del Croze stood at the edge of the surf in the early morning light staring at the eastern sky. He was concerned. Their rescue plane should have appeared from that direction a long time ago. He briefly watched the gulls and a couple of frigate birds diving for their breakfast. When he glanced back at the wooded area where many of the men still lay curled on the ground, he saw Owen Huls trudging through the heavy sands toward him. "So where the hell do you think those rescue guys are?" said Croze as Huls approached. "They shoulda been here by now. I had hoped we could get Jezewski out of here. We couldn't get the bleeding stopped last night. But, who knows, we might have lost him anyway. Do you think there's enough juice to power up the transmitter again?"

"I don't know, sir. I'll go check it out."

Croze watched Owen Huls walk on down the beach toward their plane stranded half out of water in the low tide. He prayed that he could get through to the squadron. They were in trouble here. Trouble in paradise. The nearby palms were rustling in the soft breeze. A bounty of coconuts lay scattered on the sands. Three over-turned native canoes rested on the sands beside the palms. Elsie would call them "quaint," he thought.

He smiled thinking of her and their walks together on the beaches of California where they had stayed in the Del Coronado Hotel back in January. A long time ago.

Right now the canoes seemed more ominous than quaint. He did not trust the natives who had shown up the previous evening. He had heard that many local people would try to win favor with their military occupiers in an attempt to protect their own families.

He walked back to the area where the men were just getting to their feet, brushing the sand from their clothes. They were a beat-up looking bunch, he thought. He himself felt drained physically and mentally. It had been rough last night watching Jezewski breathe his last. When he realized Jezewski was gone, he pulled the parachute canopy over his face and motioned for Igoe, who was standing nearby, to join him in a brief prayer. Afterward, while lying on the hard-packed sand of the grove, Croze had spent the rest of the night reliving the smells, the screams, the blood they had somehow survived on that horrific flight to this island.

He was just starting to look around for his officers, Wheeler and Hicks, when Calhoun pointed toward the beach. Owen Huls was floundering over the loose sand in a half-run. He was breathing hard when he reached them. "Mr. Croze—we've got Japs. Soon after I left the plane, I heard voices coming from that bunch of mangroves and bamboo you can see running inland." He pointed toward the scruffy vegetation in the distance. "I crouched down behind a palm and watched. There were eight soldiers carrying rifles. I think one had a machine gun. A couple of them boarded the plane—probably looking either for us or some equipment. After about five minutes they came out, shaking their heads. They had a short discussion and then took off back into the mangroves."

"Yeah, that doesn't sound good. What about the radio? Did you reach the squadron?"

"No go. Not even a crackle. The batteries must have discharged in the night."

"Shit." Croze had a sinking feeling. There was no doubt something had gone very wrong. The rescue plane was way over-due. "Thanks, Huls.

We need to move fast on this. I see Igoe over there. Tell him to get the men together and call in the guards."

A tired and ragged-looking crew soon gathered around Croze. "Well, men, it looks like we have company, and I don't mean friendly natives." He described Huls' encounter and warned them an attack was likely. "They can't be far away. We need to get our strategy established right now. I figure they won't come from the beach. Too open. More likely they'll approach through those trees over there where they'll have some cover. There is no telling how many there will be. One of our problems is not enough rifles or pistols for everyone. I've decided that any of you who are not armed should get out of here. Run either north or south, and we'll meet up later. Do not stay here. I don't want any dead heroes."

Charlie Moorfield passed out the weapons and ammunition they had taken from the plane. "Many of you are gunners. I know we haven't had much practice with these rifles but we have been trained on 'em. Let me know if any questions." There was silence.

Stephenson, Huls, Bumpas, and Hunt stood empty-handed, looking at the armed men. "You know what I told you," said Croze. "If you didn't receive a weapon, get ready to move out of here the moment attack begins. Stephenson - which direction do you expect to lead?"

"South," said Stephenson. "We'll be heading down the beach. Try to stick close, guys."

"If all goes well," said Croze, "we'll look for you. If we don't show up, you're on your own. There's lots of cover on the island.

The men did not have to wait long for the attack. Japanese Navy Lieutenant Yoshio Araki had arrived in the early morning with twelve armed soldiers from their small garrison in Donggala, 20 miles to the north. They were tipped off by the natives who had visited the Americans the day before. The first shot rang out a few minutes after 8:00 a.m. and struck the tree just to the right of Croze's shoulder. "Take cover, men," he yelled. "You guys without weapons get the hell out of here now." The four unarmed men ran down the beach, helping Bumpas, who was suffering from his shrapnel wounds and burns. His legs had swollen overnight, and he had a hard time keeping up. "Follow me," Huls yelled, "I think there's a swampy area on beyond the plane where we can hide. I saw it this morning."

The men ran into the mangrove swamp, crouched down in water up to their necks and covered their heads with palm fronds. "Stay close together," Stephenson whispered. "I want to be able to talk to you if I need to. Bumpas, you stay right by my side."

The armed men dashed into a palm grove. Croze, Wheeler, Hicks, and Moorfield took a position up front with Igoe, Garcia, Crow, and Calhoun, shielding the rider Donald Pell in the rear. Five Japanese soldiers charged out of the nearby brush shouting, "Banzai!" The Americans returned fire with deadly accuracy. Four of the Japanese fell. The fifth man retreated.

Then for about thirty minutes there was silence. The crew stayed hidden, waiting. Suddenly a barrage of shots rang out from the brush. Charlie Moorfield stepped from behind a tree to return fire. A bullet caught him in the chest. Looking over at Lou Wheeler with a surprised expression on his face, he moved his lips as if he was trying to speak, and then fell. John Igoe bolted toward him and was shot in the head. He fell on top of Moorfield.

"Irish! Oh my god!" Garcia yelled. "You Jap bastards, I'm going to kill every frigging one of you." He opened fire, killing three soldiers, one after the other, before ducking for cover again behind a tree. A few minutes later, Lou Wheeler took a shot in the stomach. He fell to his knees but continued to clutch his rifle. Although badly injured, he kept firing to protect his men.

The shooting continued until about 3 p.m. when it suddenly got quiet. A few minutes later, thinking the battle was over, Pell stepped from behind a tree and was shot dead. The fighting resumed. The remaining crew managed to take out more Japanese soldiers. Finally, about 5 p.m. the Japanese retreated and left the area.

For the next half-hour, the men stayed crouched behind the trees. When he finally decided it was safe, Croze went to Wheeler's side to check on his wound. "How are you doing, Lou? Let me take a look." Wheeler lifted his shirt. When Croze saw the wound in his belly, he told Wheeler he would be fine, but he knew there wasn't much chance for his survival with that type of injury. Calhoun brought the first aid kit, and Croze put a compression bandage on Wheeler's stomach. "Keep pressure on it, Lou, it will help stop the bleeding."

Joe Garcia slowly approached Igoe's body. He knelt down and turned Igoe onto his back and then reached up and closed his friend's eyes. Sadness and anger enveloped him. This wasn't the way it was supposed to end.

Croze joined Garcia and squatted down. "You okay, Garcia?"

"No, sir, I'm not. I should have done a better job shooting those friggin' gunners on that patrol boat. It might have given you a better chance to blow them out of the water."

"Don't blame yourself, Garcia, you did a great job. I'm the one that decided to go back to attack the patrol boat. If there is blame to be taken, it's all mine. Try to get some rest." When Croze left to check on Wheeler, Garcia motioned to Crow and Calhoun to follow him. They walked over to Ensign Hicks who was sitting alone on a rotting log. "Can we join you, Mr. Hicks?" Garcia asked.

"Yeah, I could use come company about now. Thanks, guys."

Wheeler began to moan. Croze lifted him into a sitting position. He sat behind him and eased Wheeler's body against his chest. "I'm cold," Wheeler whispered. Croze put his arms around him to keep him warm. He held him until Lou Wheeler stopped breathing.

Throughout the day the men in the mangrove swamps had listened to the shots with no way of knowing how many of their crew members were surviving. They were only a few feet from solid ground, and when several Japanese thudded past running, the men felt as if they could almost reach out and touch them. Stephenson was closest to the shore, and his heart was pounding so hard he was afraid the soldiers could hear it. The men exchanged glances through their palm fronds but were afraid to speak.

By 9 p.m. the men had been in the water for over twelve hours. Darkness had taken over the mangroves. A snake slithered by as the frogs and other creatures began making their eerie night sounds. Stephenson, still next to Lyle Bumpas, whispered for Huls and Hunt to come closer. They brushed the palm fronds from their heads and clustered together. "I think they're gone, at least for now, but sure as hell they'll be back in the morning. We need to decide what we are going to do. Going back to face the Japs without weapons isn't an option. We need to get out of this swamp so a rescue plane can find us. They'll never see us here," Stephenson said. He and Huls eased themselves out of the water to scout for an escape route while Hunt stayed behind to look after Bumpas.

Just before midnight, the men in the mangroves decided on a plan, one of many they had been discussing. They found the trunks of three fallen coconut palms to use for a raft. Taking off their shirts and shoes, they used the shirt sleeves and shoe laces to bind the logs together. The four men climbed onto the raft and with their hands started paddling away from the island.

When they reached the breakers about 50 yards from shore, the waves tore the raft apart and sent the men sprawling into the heavy surf. They struggled but managed to grab a single tree trunk. When they got beyond the breakers, they lifted Bumpas onto the log. His injured legs had swollen and every movement caused them to seep blood. The other three men removed their trousers and tied knots in the pant legs near the bottom. They held the trousers by the waist, lifted them over their heads and brought them down to the water line, capturing air in the legs. It was a survival trick they had learned in boot camp. "Stay close together, you guys, I don't want anyone to drift off," Stephenson warned. They continued to paddle away from the island, pushing the log with them. Keeping Bumpas on the log proved to be a full time job throughout the night. When he shifted his weight, even a little, the log rolled, pitching Bumpas into the water. During their struggles to get him back on the log, his wounds bled. They tried not to think about sharks.

Lyle Bumpas
(Compliments of Greg Bumpas)

With darkness settling, Croze gathered his men together. They took all the ammunition they had left and redistributed it. Each man had a rifle. There were three pistols but no ammunition for them. "Crow, take these pistols down to the beach and throw them into the ocean. I don't want the Japs to get them. At first light tomorrow morning, we need to look for something to use to bury our dead. We don't want to leave them lying on the ground for the scavengers."

Crow took the pistols and looked over at Garcia. "Come with me, Joe, it's dark as shit down there." The two men walked to the beach and took turns throwing the pistols into the surf.

When Garcia and Crow returned, the men gathered around in a circle and talked most of the night. The combination of adrenalin, fear, and sorrow was enough to make sure there would be no sleep tonight.

What the men did not know is that two planes from Tawi-Tawi were spending a second night looking for them. Soon after receiving the distress call from Croze's plane on June 4, a PBM-5 under the command of Lieutenant White had been in the air searching their reported position. Unable to locate the crew before running low on fuel, White had turned over the search to another PBM-5, piloted by Lieutenant Maurice Weisner. He, too, saw only an empty ocean.

CHAPTER 11

Under Attack

June 6, 1945

AT THE FIRST LIGHT OF dawn, the men clambered to their feet. They felt damp and exhausted in the heavy humidity. Insects were thick in the air. Since the water supply from the plane was nearly exhausted, Croze told them to search the nearby beach and woods for fallen coconuts as well as materials for tools they could use in burying their men.

They recovered the personal belongings of their friends and were digging graves when without warning the Japanese attacked from a position further north than that of the previous day. The men grabbed their rifles and ran for cover behind a row of palms. Before Hicks could reach safety, a bullet caught him in the back. As he spun around, another slug penetrated his left foot and a third shattered his left leg bone at the knee. He fell to the ground in a sitting position, stunned and in severe pain. Croze grabbed him under the arms and dragged him to safety behind a row of palms.

The Japanese, concealed by palms and undergrowth, continued firing at the men for an hour. Unlike the day before, they avoided stepping into the open.

"Shit, I'm out of ammo," Garcia finally yelled.

"Stay behind that palm and keep your head down," Croze shouted. Within twenty minutes, the rest of the men had used up their ammunition.

They threw down their rifles. Croze stepped out from behind a palm and held up a white handkerchief he had tied to a stick.

The Japanese hesitated, thinking it might be a trick. They soon realized, however, that the Americans could no longer fire. The soldiers stalked toward them with rifles drawn and gestured for the men to raise their hands. All did except for Hicks who was too dazed to understand the command. A soldier screamed at Hicks, but he still didn't raise his hands. The soldier kicked him in the stomach and then slammed him on the right side of his head with his rifle butt. Hicks fell face down, unconscious and bleeding from a severe skull fracture.

The soldiers gestured for Croze, Crow, Garcia, and Calhoun to follow them but to leave the injured Hicks behind. Croze refused to move without Hicks. He picked him up, put him over his shoulder, and followed the soldiers to a truck parked about a mile away. The soldiers loaded the men into the back of the truck and drove twenty miles north to their small garrison at Donggala.

When they arrived, they left the unconscious Hicks in the back of the truck. The Japanese soldiers stripped the men naked and tied their hands behind their backs. A group of soldiers from the garrison gathered around the captured men, talking and pointing. Some had never seen an American up close, or anyone as tall as Croze, and were simply curious. Others poked at the men with sticks and bayonets, taunting them.

A young skinny soldier had been looking at them from a distance. He walked up to Eddie Calhoun, punched him in the stomach, grabbed his testicles and squeezed until Calhoun screamed in pain. The soldier thought it was funny and looked over at Joe Garcia.

"Oh no," Garcia muttered under his breath, "that dirty Nip bastard ain't gonna to do that to me." The soldier approached Joe and looked him in the eyes with a grin on his face. He looked down, and as he reached out to grab him, Garcia head butted him. The soldier grunted as he hit the ground dazed.

A sergeant standing behind Garcia hit him with his rifle, knocking him on top of the dazed soldier. "Get him off of me," the soldier screamed in Japanese. The sergeant laughed, reached down, and grabbed Garcia by the arm and pulled him to his feet. The soldier got up and staggered away. He'd had enough of these captured Americans and left them alone. Garcia was happy with what he did. He got hit with a rifle, but his balls remained untouched.

An hour later the guards untied the men and ordered them to dress. Croze picked up Hicks from the back of the truck and followed the guards to a building a hundred yards away where they were shoved into a cell with one small window near the ceiling. "What's going to happen to us, Mr. Croze?" Eddie Calhoun asked.

"I think we're going to be all right. We'll probably get sent to a prisoner of war camp and with the war bound to end soon, we should be released within a few months. I'm worried about Ensign Hicks, though. He's in bad shape, and they are not offering him any medical care." He looked over at Hicks who was lying in a fetal position in the corner. He had not spoken since they arrived at Donggala.

In the evening, a guard entered the cell with five small cups of rice. He gestured for the men to eat. Kenny Crow smelled the rice and decided he didn't want it. It smelled rancid and had things in it he didn't recognize. The guard screamed at Crow and hit him with a long stick the guards always carried. When Croze protested, the guard rewarded him with a blow to his head. The guard smeared the rice on Crow's face and then threatened him with the stick until Crow took pieces of rice from his face and began eating. He retched but he kept eating.

Croze ate his rice and tried to feed some to Marshall Hicks, but he choked on it. "Water," he whispered. The guards returned with a jug of water and a pail for the men to use as a toilet. Croze was able to give Hicks a little water to wet his lips, but he was unable to swallow any.

By mid afternoon, the sun was beating down on the men at sea. They had nothing to drink since they left the plane the previous afternoon. Their shirts, used to tie the logs together, were lost in the heavy surf, and their pants were still being used for flotation. Their hats had washed away, and they were left with only their boxer shorts. Without protection, their skin burned and their lips began to dry out and crack. "I don't know how much longer I can go without water, my tongue is starting to swell," Dale Hunt said. "Where the hell is that rescue plane, doesn't the squadron give a shit about us? Are they just gonna let us die here?"

"The rescue plane will find us, I promise you," Stephenson said. "We have to keep the faith. We can't give up. Pray for rain. We all need water in a bad way."

By nightfall, Bumpas was burning with fever. His legs were infected, oozing puss and blood. He began hallucinating, rolling off of the log thinking he was at home. "Leave me alone, I'm going to my bed," he insisted.

"This isn't working," Stephenson said. "If we don't get him out of the water soon, he's going to die. All of us will die if the sharks get a sniff of that blood."

"I saw some native canoes on the beach near the plane and a bunch of coconuts on the ground," Huls said. "One of us could swim ashore and bring back coconuts, and we could put Bumpas in the canoe. We haven't heard any shooting since this morning, so the Japs may have left the area."

"I don't know," Stephenson warned. "It sounds pretty dangerous, and we're too far out for one of us to swim ashore."

"All we have to do is paddle in close to the breakers, staying out far enough so they won't suck us in. One of us can swim to the beach, grab a few coconuts and a canoe, and get back in less than an hour. Good thing you managed to keep your sheath knife, Stephy, you can open the coconuts."

"It sounds good, but who's gonna volunteer to swim ashore?" Stephenson asked.

"Not me, I almost didn't pass the swimming test in boot camp," Dale Hunt said.

"I can do it, Stephy, I'm a good swimmer," Huls said. "And I know exactly where the canoes are. Bumpas might not make it through another day."

"All right, dammit, let's go, but you got to promise to be careful, Huls."

The men paddled as close to the breakers as they dared. There was just enough light to see the plane as Huls began to swim ashore. He was tired but insisted he had enough strength to get the canoe and return. Just as he reached the beach and started walking out of the water, three Japanese soldiers, who had stayed behind to guard the plane, saw him, cocked their rifles, and yelled at him in Japanese.

Huls shouted as loudly as he could. "They've got me, they've got me." He wanted to make sure Stephenson heard him and would not follow.

The soldiers knew Huls was yelling to his friends. They ripped off his boxers and stuffed them in his mouth to keep him quiet. They beat him with the butts of their rifles. When he fell to the ground, they kicked him. "Stop, stop," Huls cried out in a muffled voice, but the men continued kicking him. One soldier kicked him in the mouth and another in the groin. Huls tried to roll into a ball. The soldiers dragged him to his feet and shoved a small spade into his hands, ordering him to dig. Each time he hesitated, they beat him. When the hole was large enough, the soldiers tied his arms and pushed him into it. Just as Huls looked up to plead for his life, they shot him to death.

Stephenson heard Huls shout and wanted to help him, but armed as he was with only a small knife, he knew any attempt would be futile. When shots rang out, the men jerked their heads and looked at each other. "Oh my God, oh my God, they shot him," Stephenson cried out. "Why the hell did I let him go. I should have stopped him or gone myself. Lord, please forgive me," he whispered.

Hungry and exhausted, his lips cracked from thirst and overcome with guilt, Stephenson sobbed as they paddled back out to sea.

Two rescue planes, flown by Lieutenants Flint and Culp, spent the day looking without success for the missing crew. Believing the plane was still at sea and on the equator, they had drawn a search area by plotting a probable drift using prevailing wind and tides. Again, their search was too far north.

CHAPTER 12

Rescue at Sea

June 7, 1945

BEFORE DAWN, THE SQUADRON COMMANDER, Lieutenant Commander Bob Harper, met with his operations officer, Lieutenant Skip Forsha, and a senior pilot, Lieutenant Morgan Saylor, to discuss their next step in the rescue efforts. They had already searched twenty-five miles south of Croze's reported position and decided to extend the search area even further. At 0630 hours, Forsha and Saylor took off from Tawi-Tawi in two PBM-5 Mariners.

Floating at sea, Stephenson, Hunt, and Bumpas caught a morning breeze that carried them a short distance westward of the island and their plane. They had had nothing to eat or drink for two days. Shortly after noon they heard an aircraft. "Oh my god, there's a plane, no wait, there are two of them, and they look like our PBMs," Hunt screamed, pounding on the log hard enough to send Bumpas sprawling into the water. As they labored to get Bumpas back on the log, his legs once again started oozing blood. They saw the planes fly on.

The two Mariners were continuing their search southward. Suddenly Ordnanceman Wally Pasco, a bow gunner in Saylor's plane, spoke, "Bow gunner to pilot, there's the beached plane, sir, about a mile ahead. Looks like the wings have been covered with something."

Morgan Saylor picked up the sighting, and called Skip Forsha on the radio. "There's the plane, Skip, just ahead on the beach. It looks like it's in good condition, but the wings have been covered with palm fronds to hide the U.S. insignias."

"I see it, Morgan, let's go down and look for survivors."

As they watched the two planes dive toward the beach, Stephenson and Hunt started screaming and yelling, waving their arms to attract attention.

"Forsha to Saylor, let's fly a pattern back and forth along the beach to look for any crew members."

"Roger, Skip, I haven't seen anyone so far," Saylor responded.

The two planes covered the entire beach area and then flew inland to look for survivors there. When the planes left the area, the men on the log were devastated. "They're leaving us, those bastards," Hunt screamed out. He looked at Stephenson who was still squinting in the direction of the disappearing planes.

"I don't know, Hunt, maybe they'll come back. Let's just hope they do."

Finding no sign of life either on the beach or in the surrounding area, the Mariner crews decided to head back to Tawi-Tawi. Soon, however, Forsha had a second thought: "Forsha to Saylor, let's go back and destroy that plane. I don't want the Japs to be able to use it for any purpose."

When they saw the planes returning, the men on the log began screaming and waving their arms. Dale Hunt took off the only piece of clothing he had left, his white boxer shorts, and started waving them in the air.

Forsha lined up for an attack. They strafed the plane and dropped a 250 pound bomb that blew the plane apart.

Just as the planes were making their final turn toward Tawi-Tawi, AMM2 W. C. Moore, the crew chief on Morgan Saylor's plane, shouted, "There are men in the water down there, Mr. Saylor!"

"Where!? I don't see anything."

The Beached Plane
(Official Navy Photograph from archives of VPB-20)

"Right there on the tip of that big reef. One of them is waving something white."

"Got them!" Saylor said. He quickly contacted Skip Forsha on the radio. "We have men down there in the water, Skip, on the tip of that large reef. One of us needs to go down and get them."

Surveying the men's situation, Forsha saw the numerous reefs in the area and knew it would be dangerous to land a plane there. "You go down, Morgan. There are a lot of reefs. I'll guide you from above.

Saylor started circling down. As he was nearing the water, Skip Forsha called out on the radio, "Morgan, hurry for God's sake, there's a huge shark, and it's swimming toward the men."

Morgan Saylor touched his plane down and taxied in the direction of the men on the log. The plane drifted to a stop about 50 yards short of the reef.

Strafing the Plane
(Official Navy Photograph from archives of VPB-20)

"You're going to have to shut down the engines, Mr. Saylor," crew chief Moore reported. "There's too much back draft to launch the rubber raft." The last thing Saylor wanted was to be dead in the water with Japanese soldiers in the area. They had likely seen the Mariners and heard the bomb blast. He advised his gunners to be on the lookout.

As the engines sputtered and shut down, Moore launched the rubber raft and started paddling toward the men on the log. Dale Hunt was still waving his skivvies and was so excited he couldn't wait. He threw his shorts up into the air and started swimming toward the raft. He swam about 15 feet when he spotted the fin coming at him. At first he thought it was a dolphin, but terror soon gripped him when he realized it was a shark. He froze as the shark swam past him, grazing him and rubbing skin from his chest and stomach.

Hunt yelled to Stephenson who was staring at him wide-eyed. He had just turned to swim back to the log when he saw the shark coming again. He raised his left arm to protect his face. The shark grabbed his arm and dragged him twenty feet under water. Hunt struggled to get loose. He hit the shark hard on its nose, but the shark didn't let go. He couldn't feel any pain, but he was running out of air, and his lungs felt as if they were going to burst. He reached his right hand into the shark's mouth and managed to free his left arm, but the razor sharp teeth tore into the tendons of the index and little fingers of his right hand.

Somehow he managed to kick himself to the surface. He floated, gasping for air, as Stephenson swam out to grab him. Moore arrived just as Stephenson got him back to the log. They loaded the dazed and bleeding Hunt for the first trip to the plane on the small raft that could take only one passenger at a time. Lyle Bumpas was next. Daulton Stephenson waited, clinging to the log, terrified that with all the splashing and blood in the water, the shark would come back. Finally, he saw the raft returning.

Stephenson was led to the crew berthing compartment where the other survivors were already put into bunks. He was hugely relieved to hear the Mariner's engines rumble to life and to feel the heavy vibration as the plane moved over the waves. Saylor taxied northward away from the reefs and, with a final kick from the jet-assisted takeoff pods, the plane lifted off. He set their course for Tawi-Tawi and turned his attention to the condition of the survivors.

In the berthing compartment, Stephenson watched as a crewman gave Hunt a morphine injection for his pain. Bumpas had one leg drawn up, and when the crewman tried to straighten it, he screamed in pain. Realizing he, too, was injured, the crew gave him morphine. They tried to start IVs to hydrate the men, but their veins were hardened from dehydration and salt water exposure. Upon getting a report of the situation, Morgan Saylor looked over at his co-pilot, Duane Roush. "Go back there and see what you can do, Duane. The men can't get the IVs started," Saylor said.

Lt(jg) Duane Roush looking aft from the cockpit of the PBM-5
(Compliments of Steve Roush)

Roush went aft as ordered, but thought, what the hell am I going to do? I've never stuck a needle in anyone. I get nervous just pinning a medal on one of my sailor's uniforms. After two attempts and two bent needles, he decided just to allow the saline to pool under the skin hoping some of it would soak in. Saylor contacted the squadron and requested a doctor be in the transfer boat when they tied up at the buoy.

During the six-hour flight to Tawi-Tawi, Saylor's crew hovered over the injured men, keeping them as comfortable as possible. With their pain relieved by the morphine injections, Bumpas and Hunt slept most of the way. Stephenson was unable to sleep. He drank water but refused food offered by the crew. He was happy to be rescued but couldn't stop thinking about Owen Huls and what he might have done to prevent his death. If only they had waited another half day, all four men would have been on the rescue plane.

When they set down on the water at Tawi-Tawi about 6 p.m., there was a whole medical team waiting in the transfer boat. They took extreme care offloading the injured men. Not waiting for other passengers, the boat departed at full speed for the USS Pokomoke. The men were taken to sick bay where Bumpas was treated for burns and infected wounds. They wheeled Dale Hunt into the operating room. The surgeons tried to save his arm, but most of the flesh and tendons in that arm had been torn away by the shark. They had no choice but to amputate his left arm above the elbow. They bandaged the two damaged fingers on his right hand and decided to wait for a specialist to address those injuries.

The following day Hunt and Bumpas were flown to a hospital ship where they remained for two days before being sent on by air transport to a navy hospital in Oakland, California.

Staying behind on the Pokomoke, Daulton Stephenson was a mental wreck. He could not sleep, had no appetite, and was depressed. The doctors found nothing physically wrong with him except dehydration and exhaustion. They gave him Nembutal to help him sleep and ordered bed rest. Bob Harper, the squadron commander, visited Stephenson in sick bay to find out what he knew about the missing crew. "I don't know very much, sir. Lieutenant Croze ordered us to run as soon as the Japs attacked because we didn't have weapons, so we headed for the swamps. We heard gun fire on two days - all day the first day and only a short while on the second. The night we arrived on the island, one of the riders died from blood loss. He had his foot blown off in the plane when the gunboat almost shot us out of the sky. I don't remember his name. I really never had a chance to talk to him."

"Can you tell me if it was Jezewski or Pell?"

"It must have been Jezewski because I remember Pell. He was alive the morning the Japs attacked. I'm sure of that."

"Is there anything else you can tell me?"

Stephenson's hands started shaking and his eyes filled with tears. "Yes, sir, there was one more. Radioman Owen Huls was with us when we escaped to sea on the log. After a day in the swamp and two days at sea, we thought Bumpas was going to die, and we didn't know how long we could live without water. Huls volunteered to swim ashore to get a native canoe and some coconuts." Stephenson stopped talking. His lower lip was quivering.

"It's all right son, take your time," Harper said, patting him on the shoulder.

After a few minutes Stephenson continued. "It's my fault, sir, I let him go, and the Japs found him. We heard him yell right after he landed on the beach and then came the shots. It just killed me that I couldn't help him. All we had between us was a small knife, and if I swam in to help, I would have been captured too. It was my responsibility to protect the other two men out there with us. I shouldn't have let him go. If only I had waited." Stephenson lowered his head.

"You did the best you could, Stephenson. You and your men came very close to losing your lives. Don't blame yourself. It was your strong leadership that kept you and the other two men alive. When you think of Huls, remember him as a hero. He gave his life to try to save his friends."

"Thank you, sir. I really appreciate the talk, Commander Harper."

"I'm sending you home for a rest. We can transfer you to a crew that is leaving in three days to fly back to the States. When you arrive in California, you can go home on a thirty-day recuperation leave. Get a good rest, spend time with your family, and try not to think about the war. At the end of your leave, you'll receive transfer orders."

"Thank you, sir, I can't tell you how much I appreciate that. I thought I would never see my wife again." Stephenson returned to his bed and tried not to think about anything but his wife, Jewel. He said a prayer and fell asleep.

On the day that the Mariner crews rescued the three men from the sea, Croze and his three crewmen were loaded onto a truck and driven from Donggala to a larger Japanese garrison in the town of Palu, twenty miles northeast. When they arrived, the uninjured men were put in a large cell area where guards untied their arms and allowed them to walk around. There were no other prisoners in the cell with them.

They took the badly wounded Ensign Marshall Hicks to the base dispensary, removed his blood-stained uniform, and put him in a bed, covering him with a dirty sheet. They left a glass of water on the table next to him. When they left the room, they locked the door and gave the medical staff strict orders that Hicks was not to be given either food or medical attention. The local Indonesian doctor begged the Japanese to allow him to treat Hicks, but they refused and threatened him with death if he disobeyed their orders. Every day Croze asked a guard who spoke a little English about Marshall Hicks. "Man in hospital," was all the guard could tell him.

The guards allowed the four men to exercise every other day. They gave them an old baseball that had a torn jacket and let them play stick ball in the field outside the jail. Four armed guards kept a close eye on the men. They acted stern and threatening, but they cheered when one of the men got a hit.

Jewel and Daulton Stephenson
(Compliments of Donna Stephenson Dennison)

In the infirmary, Marshall Hicks slept most of the day. At night he was haunted by visions and terrifying nightmares. He could feel maggots nibbling at the wounds on his foot and knee and screamed for help, but got no answer. Once a day an orderly was allowed to enter his room to refill the water glass but didn't speak and tried not to look him in the eye. Hicks wanted to tell him his bed was wet with urine. He moved his lips, but no sound came out.

CHAPTER 13

Operation Raven, the Search for the Missing Crew

June 8, 1945

AFTER HIS INTERVIEW WITH STEPHENSON, Lieutenant Commander Bob Harper and his staff worked through the night to get the Missing in Action notices ready to be sent to the families. The process was tedious because each notice had to be routed through the chain of command to the Bureau of Naval Personnel in Washington. The telegrams went out to the families on June 12th.

Ensign Lewis Wheeler's wife, Betty, was among those receiving the notice sent by Western Union that her husband was missing in action. It read in part, "Your great anxiety is appreciated, and you will be furnished details when received." Unfortunately, the missing detail was that Wheeler was already deceased, killed in the fire-fight on the morning of June 5th. Betty Jean kept the notice for years until it finally went out to the curb in an old suitcase among other debris cleared from the house when it was sold and she moved away.

The Squadron Commander did not abandon the search for the men. He immediately sent a request for help to the Allied Intelligence Bureau (AIB) on Morotai Island. The Z Special Unit of the Australian Army took

Fatal Error

> **WESTERN UNION**
>
> C161 46 GOVT=WASHINGTON DC 12 807P
>
> MRS BETTY JANE WHEELER=
>
> 512 VAIL ST MICHIGANCITY IND=
>
> I DEEPLY REGRET TO INFORM YOU THAT YOUR HUSBAND ENSIGN LEWIS ALBERT WHEELER USNR IS MISSING IN ACTION WHILE IN THE SERVICE OF HIS COUNTRY. YOUR GREAT ANXIETY IS APPRECIATED AND YOU WILL BE FURNISHED DETAILS WHEN RECEIVED. TO PREVENT POSSIBLE AID TO OUR ENEMIES PLEASE DO NOT DIVULGE THE NAME OF HIS SHIP OR STATION UNLESS THE GENERAL CIRCUMSTANCES ARE MADE PUBLIC IN NEWS STORIES=
>
> VICE ADMIRAL RANDALL JACOBS THE CHIEF OF NAVAL PERSONNEL

Western Union Telegram
(Original Telegram in the suitcase found by Betty Morris)

on the job of searching for the missing crew. The Unit was an elite group, the toughest and most highly trained in the Australian army. After years of action in the Pacific war, they were experienced in espionage, jungle warfare, and special weapons.

The Z Special Unit dubbed their mission Operation Raven, a name borrowed from one of their members. Sergeant Raven, Sergeant Keneally, and Corporal Philpott served on the team headed by Lieutenant Scobell McFerran-Rogers. Captain Keith Stringfellow was their planning officer. A Celebes native, Roestan, an interpreter for the Australian Army, took on the job of communicating with local people.

Operation Raven launched on June 11, one week after Croze's plane went down in the Celebes. With official permission from General MacArthur, the American squadron picked up the Z Special team from

Morotai Island and flew them to Tawi-Tawi where they could gain further information about the area and the last known situation of the crew.

Meanwhile, Ensign Marshall Hicks was nearing death in the Japanese dispensary in Palu. He was having difficulty breathing. His lips and mouth were dry, but he did not have the strength to reach for the water glass. He wished the orderly would come in to help him. A little after noon, he slipped into a coma and died the evening of June 12th, a few hours before the nightly visions and nightmares returned. The dispensary staff buried him the next morning in the hospital cemetery with a marker that said "American Pilot."

Two days after their arrival on Tawi-Tawi, the Australian search team was ready to explore the location where Croze's plane was stranded. Sighting the bombed-out plane on the island shore, McFerran-Rogers had his team lined up at the hatch in the after compartment, ready to launch their raft and paddle ashore. Pilot Lieutenant Phillips cut the engines and the plane drifted to a stop. One at a time the Australian search team stepped out of the after-compartment hatch and into the raft.

Their day's mission ended abruptly. They had paddled only a short ways from the rear of the plane when Lieutenant Phillips started the engines. The prop wash was so strong it overturned the raft, spilling the men and their gear into the ocean. The team lost all their equipment including guns, weapons, and radios. One of the men was pulled under water by the weight of his gun and strapped-on hand grenades. Struggling to drop the equipment, he felt the panic of drowning. Finally, desperate for a breath of air, he got free and fought his way back to the surface. The team returned to Tawi-Tawi.

The following day, the resupplied team boarded a plane piloted by Lieutenant Morgan Saylor and went ashore in the area of Croze's beached PBM-5. They came across a local person who knew something about the missing men. He told the interpreter, Roestan, that he had found one of the men: "He was dead under a parachute canopy. I buried him right over there where you see that mound of fresh dirt." He said the Japanese captured four men and took them away, but he had no further information. He denied knowing about the four men killed in action by the Japanese soldiers. With no additional findings, the Raven team returned to Tawi-Tawi.

The Allied Intelligence Bureau determined that they needed a larger, more heavily armed party to go deeper into enemy territory on the island to locate and rescue the missing airmen. After flying additional men and equipment into Tawi-Tawi to reinforce the team, they made plans to stay ashore at least one night and expand the search area. Major Tony Gluth was the newly assigned leader with McFerran-Rogers as assistant. Corporals Leahy, Fawkes, Hopkins and Private Whitworth were added to the team. Corporal Philpott, a member of the original team, had to drop out because of illness.

On June 19th, fifteen days after Croze's crew reached the Celebes, the expanded search party left Tawi-Tawi at 0115 hours. Lieutenant Saylor delivered the team to an area north of the beached plane where they went ashore at 0715. Crew Chief Moore and another member of Saylor's crew accompanied them, waiting with the raft for a few hours just in case the Aussies needed to make a quick departure. After three hours with no signs of trouble, the two men from the Mariner crew rowed back to the plane for the return flight to Tawi-Tawi.

During their first three hours on the island, the Raven party found a dozen natives to interview. None admitted to having information about the missing airmen. When the interpreter tried to persuade two of the natives to return with them to Tawi-Tawi, they refused. Finally, the Australians tried to convince them with a show of force. The frightened natives burst into tears.

"Bloody hell," Major Gluth yelled, "let the buggers be. They're not going to come with us unless we tie them up and drag them kicking and screaming."

At 1100 hours, the team began a three hour trek through soft sand and heavy undergrowth and finally arrived at the village of Sodi at 1400. There they found only residents who were so frightened of Japanese reprisals that they refused to speak at all during the interrogation. One man told Roestan that the Japanese would kill them and their entire village if they spoke even one word.

Giving up on the people of Sodi, Gluth pushed on further north for several hours, arriving in the village of Lalombi at 1730 hours. They approached four houses situated along a river bank, probably the homes of fishermen. The people who came out to meet them were nervous, but after discovering they could talk with Roestan in their own language, they began to relax. They boiled water so the Australians could make tea and gave them mats to sit on for their tea break.

Fifteen minutes later, while finishing their tea, the team observed four men in a cart pulled by a water buffalo on the opposite side of the river. They were about to cross the river when they spotted the Australians. Making a quick turn in the opposite direction, they whipped the buffalo to leave as fast as possible. One of the men in the cart appeared to be wearing a U. S. Navy dungaree shirt. Another wore a navy issue white undershirt.

Gluth decided that he would make a thorough investigation of the other side of the river, taking along Roestan, their interpreter, and Private John Whitworth, a world class swimmer and former life guard at Coogee Beach in Sydney. Their trip proved futile. On the opposite bank, they searched thirty houses. All were empty. Not a single living person to be seen. The entire village had faded into the jungle when they saw the men swimming across the river. In one of the houses, however, they discovered a small piece of Croze's wrecked PBM-5 Mariner and a pair of navy issue sun glasses.

About 1900 hours, the men gave up and swam back to join the rest of their party. With darkness approaching, Gluth decided that nothing would be gained by attempting to move north or south. He and his team

Fatal Error

bedded down for the night on the river bank to await the scheduled arrival of the PBM-5 Mariner in the morning.

The next morning, however, the Japanese arrived before the plane. At about 0900, Major Gluth heard voices, and then saw six Japanese soldiers emerging from the brush. As the Raven team dived for cover in a shallow tidal marsh, the Japanese opened fire. Lieutenant Scobell McFerran-Rogers, stepping into the open for a good shot, was cut down by machine gun fire. Corporal Henry Fawkes ran to McFerran-Roger's side and attempted to pull him to safety. As soon as he grabbed the lieutenant, McFerran-Rogers died. Fawkes snatched up his identity discs and his Bren gun. In the next instant, the interpreter, Roestan, was shot and killed.

Gluth kept glancing through the dense branches of mangroves along the shoreline, hoping for the arrival of their PBM-5 Mariner. Finally, he saw the plane splashing down and a rubber raft launching toward the beach. He hailed his men and yelled for them to head through the undergrowth, turn onto the beach, and run into the water as far out as possible. As the men dashed for the shoreline, Gluth held back, flinging hand grenades at the Japanese. On his command, all the men, except for Private John Whitworth, turned and ran into the water toward the approaching rubber raft. The team hauled them aboard and rowed to the plane. Whitworth was missing. One of the men remembered seeing him holding his side, uncertain if he was wounded or adjusting his equipment. Another man recalled hearing Whitworth shout, "Wait a minute," but he had not made it to the raft. Once airborne, the plane flew up and down the beach area searching for Private John Whitworth, but they never saw him again.

The surviving members of the Raven team flew to Tawi-Tawi and a day later returned to their base on Morotai. They later learned that John Whitworth tried to evade the enemy but was captured the following day on June 21st. He was executed on July 1, 1945.

Private John Whitworth
(Compliments of Sally Olander)

CHAPTER 14

In Custody of the Kempei Tai

June 25, 1945

DEL CROZE AND THE THREE remaining crewmen - Joe Garcia, Kenny Crow, and Eddie Calhoun - were still being held in the Japanese garrison's jail at Palu, North Celebes. So far, treatment by their Japanese captors had not been cruel. Although their food was distasteful, it was adequate to maintain their health. They were allowed to exercise and were not tied while in their cell. This was about to change, and they would soon find themselves in a living hell.

Colonel Michinori Nakamura, Commander of the Kempei Tai Headquarters in Singkang, South Celebes, asked that the Americans be transferred to his command so he could interrogate them. The Kempei Tai was an organization similar to the German Gestapo, but far more brutal. Ordinary Japanese soldiers were afraid of them. The Kempei Tai believed that torture was a part of interrogation and did not hesitate to use it often and with great force.

With no roads to connect the north of Celebes to the south, the men went by truck, then by sea, and again by truck to reach their destination of Singkang.

They arrived in Singkang on July 2, 1945, and stopped in front of the Second Army Headquarters. An eye witness, Dr. Stamford Rampen, a veterinary surgeon whose office was across the street from the headquarters building, observed their arrival. Four Americans and nine Japanese guards were in the back of the truck. Del Croze, wearing a long-sleeved khaki uniform and khaki hat, sat in the center, facing the rear of the truck. He had a four or five day growth of beard and appeared to be in good health. Three men were sitting on the side of the truck facing Dr. Rampen's office. First was the very young looking Eddie Calhoun, with no growth of beard at all, then Kenny Crow with light brown hair and a five day growth, and third was Joe Garcia with a full head of black hair and a five day growth. All the men appeared to be in good health with no marks or bruises that the doctor could see. Their uniforms had no rips or tears.

Although the Second Army Headquarters at Singkang had a jail, the guards led the men to the Kempei Tai Headquarters, a frame structure with a small jail on the ground level.

The guards lined up the men outside the jail with their hands tied behind them and kept them standing for over an hour. When a sergeant arrived, he ordered the guards to untie the men. "Now you take off clothes," the sergeant ordered. The guards poked at them with sticks until they were naked. Forcing the men onto their knees, the guards beat them with sticks the size of baseball bats until they were covered with welts. Kenny Crow took a blow to the side of his head that caused his left eye to swell shut. Crow yelled at the guard who hit him. The guard rewarded him with a kick to his groin, doubling him up in pain. They warned the men that if any one of them tried to escape, they would all be executed.

They took their uniforms away and gave them Japanese trousers and t-shirts to wear. There were no trousers even close to fitting the six foot two inch Croze, so they allowed him to wear his uniform trousers. He squeezed into one of the t-shirts. They tied the men with their hands behind them and put them in separate rooms in the jail, a large area partitioned by hanging straw mats. The men were left without socks or shoes and ordered not to speak to one another. When Croze asked for water for his men, the guards refused.

Kempei Tai Headquarters at Singkang with Jail on Ground Floor
(Photo in suitcase found by Betty Morris)

Exhausted and in extreme pain, the men collapsed onto the floor in their cells. Without bunks or blankets, they slept on the cold cement floor separated from each other by thin walls. The floor smelled of mildew and the straw mats reminded the men of a wet dog. Croze wanted to protect his crew and was in agony every time he heard their moans or occasional sobs.

The men were given nothing to eat or drink until the following afternoon. The guards scooped two tablespoons of rice from a bucket and put it on the floor in front of them. With their hands tied behind them, they had to lean down and eat like dogs. They lapped up water with their tongues from a small dish. The men were fed like this twice a day. Each time the guards entered their cells, they struck the men with long sticks, often breaking the skin.

On July 5th, three days after the men had arrived in Singkang, Colonel Nakamura called his assistant, Major Toshitake Odamura, to his office and directed him to prepare a list of questions to ask the American airmen. Nakamura advised Odamura that an English speaking interpreter had just arrived and that he was to make the arrangements to interrogate the prisoners right away.

After drafting the list of questions, Major Odamura ordered the guards to bring the men one at a time to his office above the jail. Waiting in the office for the prisoners was the interpreter, Sergeant Tokujiro Kato. Kato was born and raised in southern California and lived there until his family returned to Japan when he was twelve years old. He was drafted into the Japanese army on March 10, 1941. Because Kato spoke fluent English, they sent him to the Kempei Tai as an interpreter. Unlike most of the Kempei Tai, Kato was not a brutal or vengeful man, and he felt an attachment to his former home and affection for the American people.

The guards delivered Croze to Kato with his hands tied behind his back. Kato dismissed the guard, untied Croze, and asked him to be seated. "Good afternoon, Croze, can you tell me your rank please."

"I am a navy lieutenant."

"What kind of plane were you flying, what was your job on the plane, and how did you end up in the Celebes?"

"I was flying a PBM-5 Mariner. I am the patrol plane commander, and we were shot down over the Makassar Strait."

"Yes, well we know about your plane. What is your home base?"

"I am stationed at Tawi-Tawi in the Philippines."

"Think about this very carefully, Croze. We need to know if the Americans or their allies have any plans to make a ground invasion of the Celebes."

"I don't believe so. We have never been told anything about invading the Celebes."

"Thank you, Croze, I have no further questions."

"Tell me please, how is it that you speak English perfectly without a trace of accent?"

"Well, I was born in Brawley, California, 125 miles east of San Diego and not far from the Mexican border. I grew up and went to school there. My father was a foreman for a large vegetable farm in the Imperial Valley. When the depression hit, my parents lost their jobs, so we returned to Japan. I was drafted into the army in 1941."

"So you are an American citizen."

"Yes, technically. I'm an American citizen by birth, but I consider myself to be a Japanese citizen. Japan doesn't recognize my American citizenship. Tell me your first name, Croze, and tell me a little about yourself."

"My name is DeLand, but everyone calls me Del. I grew up in Minnesota and went to college in North Dakota where I played on the football team and was on the wrestling team. I am married to a wonderful woman named Elsie."

"Well, my name is Tokujiro, but the kids in school had a hard time pronouncing it so they all called me Zero. I was also an athlete and played baseball in school."

"Thank you, Tokujiro, I am glad to meet you, but I must protest about the treatment my men are getting. We are starving with only a few tablespoons of rice a day. Our hands are always tied behind us, and it is very difficult to eat, and we are beaten several times a day for no apparent reason. I haven't even been allowed to talk to my men to see if they are all right. Can you help us, please?"

"I will do what I can, but no promises."

Kato summoned the guards who tied Croze's hands behind his back and returned him to his small cell.

One by one, Crow, Garcia, and Calhoun were brought up to the Kempei Tai Headquarters to be interrogated by Kato. After speaking with Croze, he knew the other men would not have any new information. He untied each man to make him feel comfortable. He asked them to describe their job on the plane and then moved the conversations to a more personal nature. Kato had always dreamed of having his own car and was fascinated by the story Kenny Crow told of rebuilding the engine of his Plymouth all by himself. He was also interested in Joe

Garcia's stories of hunting and fishing along the Nueces River, something Kato never had the opportunity to do. Kato had learned Morse code as a Boy Scout in California. When he heard that Eddie Calhoun was a radioman, he asked him to spell the name Calhoun slowly, using only dots and dashes.

Once the interviews were completed, the men were removed from their individual cells and allowed to mingle. They discovered there was another American in the jail with them, an Army Air Forces fighter pilot. He told the new arrivals his fighter plane had been shot down near Pozo, and he had been captured after hiding in the jungle for a week. (*Numerous efforts have been made to identify this fighter pilot, but, unfortunately, his identity remains unknown.*)

They also became friends with a young Indonesian man named Makham Isa, who was in the Kempei Tai jail for murder and desertion. Isa had been conscripted into the Japanese army as a "heiho" boy, a non-combatant auxiliary soldier who did menial chores. Isa hated the Japanese and escaped. In order to get away, he killed a Kempei Tai guard. The men talked to Isa using sounds and often had to turn their backs to use their hands when trying to explain something.

Although Sergeant Kato saw the men and talked with them every day, he wasn't able to help them. Croze asked Kato if he could find a job for the men so they wouldn't have to remain tied in a small room every day, but Kato said that was impossible.

Once a week the American prisoners were taken for a walk. Before the walks began, the men were required to pay their respects to Emperor Hirohito by bowing deeply in the direction of Tokyo. Their hands were still tied behind their backs with an attached length of rope that was tied around their ankles. This method of trussing would cause a man to fall if he attempted to run. The local Indonesian people watched these weekly walks with interest and noted how every week the Americans appeared to be thinner and weaker. During one of these walks, the fighter pilot tripped and fell. He had to be helped back to the jail after the guards viciously beat him.

Near the end of July, Tokujiro Kato came to visit Croze one last time. He told him he was leaving for a base in the north of Celebes. Kato told Croze he had no idea what the Kempei Tai planned to do with the prisoners but tried to reassure him that there were no plans to execute them.

Knowing the war was coming to an end, Kato told Croze he and his crew should be home very soon. He apologized for his inability to make life easier for Croze and his men and wished them all the best for the future. Kato wrote his name and his address in Japan on a piece of paper and put it in Croze's pocket. "Contact me after the war is over, Del, and maybe I can visit you in Minneapolis," he said.

"Okay, 'Zero.' See you in Minnesota. I'll take you to a baseball game," Croze replied with a grin.

The Kempei Tai jail guards were irritated that Sergeant Kato liked Croze and the other Americans. After Kato left Singkang, the guards made life even harder for the prisoners. They were beaten more frequently and were sometimes made to wait an hour after requesting a visit to the latrine. Life had become even more difficult for the Americans.

Veterinary surgeon, Stamford Rampen, who had witnessed the arrival of the Americans in Singkang, happened to see Joe Garcia one day in the yard outside the jail. Although several weeks had passed, he remembered Garcia because he was the only American with a full head of black hair.

Rampen was driving his car to work about 9 a.m. Just as he approached the building where the men were being held, he saw Garcia standing in the yard. A Japanese guard stood next to him, there was no one else in the yard. He noticed that Garcia had a heavier growth of beard. He was wearing a white t-shirt and a pair of Japanese trousers and appeared to be in very poor physical condition. Rampen did not notice any blood or bandages on Garcia. Joe stood still and was looking directly at Rampen. Just as he passed the jail, Rampen nodded and Garcia nodded in return. He wanted very much to speak with the young American, but he knew the guard would not permit it.

On July 20th, Colonel Nakamura decided to use one of the American prisoners for propaganda purposes, since he was no longer getting any intelligence from them. Late one afternoon, he called his adjutant, Lieutenant Kotaro Kamisuki, to his office and told him his plans.

"Which prisoner do you want to use?" Kamisuki asked.

"I can't tell one from the other," Nakamura replied. "I only know that one is very big and one is very small. Use the small one."

The following day Lieutenant Kamisuki, accompanied by Warrant Officer Kunio Matsumoto, went to the Kempei Tai jail and spoke to the senior guard. They handed the guard a pair of white Japanese pajamas and then pointed to Joe Garcia.

"Clean him up, and I mean scrub him good. When you're done put him in these pajamas and deliver him to my office. And you had better make him look good," Kamisuki ordered the guard. The guard acknowledged, and he and the other guards bowed as the officers left the jail.

Two of the junior guards heated water in large buckets and went to their bath house to get the brushes and scrapers they used for bathing. They took Joe Garcia into the yard behind the jail, stripped him, and tied his hands loosely behind him. They scrubbed him from head to toe, using a scrub brush on his elbows, knees, and feet. They used wooden scrapers to remove the dried skin from his body. They trimmed his hair and shaved him, leaving only a moustache and a Van Dyke beard. Joe shivered when they rinsed him with two buckets of cold water. After he had put on the Japanese pajamas and combed his hair, they delivered him to the Adjutant—clean and freshly groomed.

Lieutenant Kamisuki was pleased. "Leave him with me," Kamisuki said, "and send the photographer to the Colonel's office."

That evening, the Kempei Tai hosted a dinner at the Officer's Club in Singkang. They invited about forty local Indonesians and several Japanese officers to attend. The veterinarian, Dr. Rampen, received an invitation and attended the dinner.

After dinner, a Japanese Captain spoke while they handed out a photograph to each guest. Rampen recognized the man in the photograph as the black haired American, Joe Garcia. He was dressed in white Japanese-style pajamas, had no shoes or hat, and had long black hair. He was clean-shaven except for a mustache and a three-inch long Van Dyke beard. Rampen noticed that Garcia appeared to be in very poor physical condition and his eyes lacked luster. After handing out the picture, the Japanese Captain told the guests that this was an example of a white man who had been captured. The photo, he said, should assure Indonesians that they could easily capture the white men.

The Captain then passed around another picture of this same American prisoner. He allowed the guests to look at it but said they had to return it. The second photograph was of Joe Garcia, shirtless without the pajama top. This time he was on the ground, flat on his back, with his legs spread apart. An Indonesian boy was kneeling by Garcia's side with his knee on Garcia's chest. The boy had his right fist raised up as if to punch him in the face. His left hand clutched Garcia by the throat.

After the photographs were taken, Garcia was delivered back to the jail cell in his regular Japanese clothes. He was visibly upset and shaking with anger when he returned. He told the guys what had happened. "The guards took me out and scrubbed me. Those bastards wouldn't even let me wash my own balls. They scraped me so hard with those wooden scrapers that I thought I was going to start bleeding. When they sharpened the straight razor, I thought they were going to cut my throat. They made me sit on a stool, and I was nervous as hell when they started shaving me. I wanted to do it myself, but they wouldn't let me. They made me put on some Jap pajamas and took me to the Colonel's office."

"What happened when you got there?" Eddie Calhoun asked.

"They took me to different places and took a bunch of pictures of me. Some just standing there looking stupid and some with an Indonesian kid, about twelve years old, looking like he was trying to kill me. They let the kid hit me a few times. He thought it was fun. Then they took me outside and took pictures with a bunch of Jap soldiers surrounding me. In some of the pictures they made me sit naked on the ground with a soldier pointing his rifle at me." Joe was silent for a minute and then continued, "They took pictures with Jap soldiers poking me with their bayonets. They were all laughing and thought it was very funny."

Unlike the American prisoners, Makham Isa did not have his hands tied behind his back. Joe gestured for Isa to pull up his t-shirt. "Take a look at this on my chest where one of those Jap bastards stuck me with his bayonet and broke the skin."

The men gathered around Garcia to cheer him up. "Don't worry about me, guys, I'm okay." Garcia said. "They didn't hurt me very much. It just pissed me off royally that my hands were tied and I couldn't fight back. I could have beat the crap out of any one of those slant-eyed bastards."

Joe Garcia walked over to the corner and sat down. He closed his eyes and began to relax. "You all right, Joe?" Kenny Crow asked. "Need some company?"

"No thanks, Kenny, I'm okay. I just need to be alone so I can mentally escape this hell hole for a little while. I'll talk to you later."

When he finally relaxed, Joe imagined himself back in Texas. He was walking along the Nueces River with his brother Richard. The little guy hadn't learned to walk yet. He was just eleven months old and was sitting on Joe's shoulders. "Come on, little brother, I'm gonna show you one of my favorite places in the whole world."

CHAPTER 15

The Execution

July 27, 1945

FOR THE NEXT THREE WEEKS, the treatment of the prisoners was unbearable. Their ration of rice was cut to the point of starvation. One of the men had become sick, according to later testimony. The Japanese refused to give him medicine or any kind of medical treatment. There were no more exercise walks, and the men were weak and exhausted. The beatings continued with no let up. Having their hands tied in front instead of behind them was their only relief now.

On July 27th, Colonel Nakamura sent his second in command, Major Odamura, to the Second Army Headquarters to see Lieutenant Colonel Ishiro. Nakamura wanted to get rid of the American prisoners, and it was Ishiro's duty to determine when a prisoner was no longer valued as a source of intelligence. Odamura returned without a definite answer.

"What do you mean he didn't give you an answer?" Nakamura asked.

"Well, at first he said we could send them to Watampone POW camp, but then he said there were no vehicles available to transport the prisoners. He whispered to me that we could just dispose of them."

"What is 'dispose of them' supposed to mean? Send them away or execute them?"

"I'm not sure what he meant, Colonel, but I'll go back and talk to him again."

On August 2, 1945, Odamura returned to the Second Army headquarters to visit with Lieutenant Colonel Ishiro. This time the answer was unequivocal: have the men executed as soon as possible. "When I asked if it wouldn't be better to send them to Java, since International Law is against execution without a court martial, he just ignored me," Odamura told Colonel Nakamura. "He said that war conditions made it impossible to take any action other than to execute the men."

"All right, Major, draw up the execution plan and give it to me by tomorrow."

"Yes, sir, I'll have the plans in your office by tomorrow morning."

Odamura did not want to draw up the plans. He called Warrant Officer Matsumoto and directed him to write them.

On the morning of August 3rd, Warrant Officer Matsumoto walked to the Kempei Tai jail. He was carrying the clothes taken from the prisoners when they arrived. He told the men to put on their uniforms and prepare to be transferred to the Second Army jail later that day.

The Indonesian boy, Makham Isa, who had been imprisoned with the Americans, noticed that the demeanor of the men changed when they received these orders. They quietly whispered among themselves, and although they remained friendly, they did not try to communicate with him. It was clear that the men suspected what was coming. Later that evening, just before dark, Matsumoto and four guards marched the American prisoners to the Second Army jail.

"What do you think, Mr. Croze, are they going to kill us or send us to a prisoner of war camp?" Kenny Crow asked.

"I can't be sure, Crow, but we know the Japs are mad as hell about the U.S. firebombing of Tokyo that has been going on for the past few months. I don't think they are in the mood to do us any favors. Whatever happens, we need to face it with strength and dignity."

Early the next morning, August 4, 1945, Matsumoto entered the Second Army jail with two armed guards. They took the five American prisoners and marched them along a path into a wooded area and had them wait by a large tree. Matsumoto left Sergeant Major Shigeo Ichihashi and Sergeant Kazuaki Okazaki to guard the prisoners.

Path to the Wooded Area
(Photo in suitcase found by Betty Morris)

About fifty yards beyond the point where the men were waiting, was a large grave that had been dug the previous afternoon. Standing around the grave were Colonel Michinori Nakamura; his assistant, Major Toshitake Odamura; the adjutant, Lieutenant Kotaro Kamisuki; and Sergeants Rinji Sasakura and Koshin Ichijo. All of them were wearing swords, the long, leather-wrapped helves projecting from their scabbards. A light rain had begun to fall, and a private, Fumiyuki Kazato, arrived with rain coats for the officers. He decided to stay and watch the proceedings.

Warrant Officer Matsumoto bowed and reported to the Colonel, "We are ready, sir."

"Send the big one first," Nakamura said.

Sergeant Major Ichihashi blind folded Croze, led him to the rim of the grave, and made him kneel. Ichihashi returned to the waiting area.

The colonel had selected his favorite sergeant, Rinji Sasakura, to execute Croze. Sasakura walked over to Croze and adjusted one of his knees. He drew his sword, poured water on the slender, twenty-four-inch long curving blade, and raised it above his head. Sasakura brought the sword down with great force onto Croze's neck and beheaded him. He tumbled into the grave.

"Send that little one next," the colonel ordered.

Sergeant Okazaki blind-folded Joe Garcia, led him to the grave's edge, and shoved him into a kneeling position. The colonel selected another favorite, Sergeant Koshin Ichijo, to execute Garcia. Ichijo unsheathed his sword. Stepping to the side of the kneeling man, he clasped the sword helve in both hands and raised the blade. Garcia's body fell onto Croze's in the grave below.

Next, Warrant Officer Matsumoto decided to do the honors himself and executed the fighter pilot who had been incarcerated with Croze's crew.

Matsumoto had planned to use only Kempei Tai soldiers to perform the executions, but four guards from the Second Army jail who had joined the party were looking anxious and talking among themselves. Matsumoto asked if any of them wished to execute one of the Americans.

Fatal Error

First, a skinny sergeant stepped forward. He executed Kenny Crow. He was followed by a fat warrant officer who executed Eddie Calhoun.

The officers left the area and the enlisted men covered the grave. To make sure the grave which contained evidence of war crimes would never be found, the men covered it with dried leaves and branches. They left the area, went to breakfast, and bragged about how well they had performed the executions of the Americans.

Two days later, on August 6, the Enola Gay dropped an atomic bomb on Hiroshima.

Camouflaged Mass Grave
(Photo in suitcase found by Betty Morris)

CHAPTER 16

End of the War

August 14, 1945

WORD OF THE JAPANESE SURRENDER reached Colonel Michinori Nakamura's Kempei Tai headquarters in Singkang by telegraph within a few hours. The news was not a surprise to the high ranking officers, but many of the enlisted soldiers were still under the impression that Japan could win the war.

The Japanese at Singkang had been stunned by the news that atomic bombs destroyed the cities of Hiroshima and Nagasaki. Many of the soldiers had no concept how a single bomb could destroy a city. Their ultimate shock came when the voice of the Emperor was broadcast. No common Japanese citizen had ever heard the voice of this royal human who they believed was descended from a god. The angry and disappointed soldiers had some relief when the Japanese government announced that surrendering under the terms of a ceasefire would not be considered a loss of honor as defined by the Bushido code that demanded fighting to the death.

The soldiers at Singkang would have a long wait to be repatriated. They had no ships or airplanes and were stuck on the large island of Celebes with no choice but to wait for the Allied armies to arrive. Renji Sasakura, the sergeant who executed Del Croze, decided to make his usual frequent visit to the comfort station to bury his sorrow with sake and a woman, only to discover all the women had disappeared overnight. When the news of the surrender reached the brothels, the women fled fearing for their lives. Many of them were taken in by Indonesian families, who hid them until the Allied troops arrived.

Within a few days, the Dutch army began to reestablish their territories taken by the Japanese at the beginning of the war and arrived in force at Singkang. The Japanese soldiers were stripped of their clothes and made to wait in an open field until their barracks were thoroughly searched and all weapons, including personal swords, were confiscated. The local Indonesian people, angry and frustrated by their constant fear of the Japanese, were happy to point out soldiers they knew had committed war crimes.

On November 6, 1945, Flight Lieutenant Martin O'Shea, a representative of the Casualty Section of the Royal Australian Air Forces, arrived in Singkang and was led to the American crew's mass grave by Doctor Djanharajah Yenie, an Indonesian surgeon from the local leper hospital. One of his patients, the owner of the property where the grave was located, happened to take a walk and discovered the freshly dug grave the afternoon before the execution. The patient confided in Doctor Yenie, but they both remained silent until they were sure the war was over.

The Australians exhumed the bodies from the mass grave and identified them as Americans. They then wrapped them in Australian blankets, re-interred them, and notified the American authorities.

Then, six months later, on May 28, 1946, the U.S. Graves Registration Service, working in the area where the PBM-5 had been beached, advised the families that the bodies of five men had been discovered near there. The remains of Robert Jezewski, John Igoe, Donald Pell, and Charles Moorfield as well as the remains of Marshall Hicks, buried in Palu, were exhumed and identified using dental charts. After notifying the families, the Registration Service flew the bodies to Calcutta, India, for burial in a temporary national cemetery there.

The Graves Registration team finally arrived in Singkang on August 24, 1946, to recover the bodies of Del Croze, Joe Garcia, Kenny Crow, and Eddie Calhoun. They used dental charts to establish definite identity and then flew the remains to Calcutta, India, where they were buried at Barrackpore National Cemetery.

The body of Owen Huls, who was shot to death and buried on the beach, was never found. Of the eleven men on the plane who lost their lives, Huls was the only crew member whose remains were not recovered.

In early 1948, the bodies were returned to the United States and shipped to their respective home towns for burial. DeLand Croze and Robert Jezewski were buried at the National Cemetery of the Pacific in Honolulu, Hawaii.

With information provided by Makham Isa, the young man who had been imprisoned with the crew members, and by several Indonesian workers and local citizens, the Japanese soldiers responsible for the execution were identified and sent to a military prison in Manila, Philippines, awaiting trial.

The trial was held before a United States Military Commission at the former High Commissioner's Residence, Manila, on January 24, 1947, and was completed on February 13, 1947. The Prosecutor was Emory C. Smith, a former naval officer, who had conducted a three month investigation in Singkang, Celebes, prior to the trial. The Chief Defense Council was Mr. Benjamin L. Levi.

Although Colonel Nakamura advised the men not to talk about the execution, his words went unheeded. When they were on the stand, they readily told the story as they remembered it. All of the soldiers who participated in the execution admitted their part and implicated other members of the Kempei Tai who were involved.

The members of the tribunal concluded that each of the participants in the execution was guilty. Sentences were determined by their level of culpability and were handed down pending the trial review. During the review, a motion was made to dismiss the charges against Sasakura, Ichijo, Kazato, Ichihashi and Okazaki on the grounds that they acted in obedience to superior orders. The motion was denied, but the tribunal concluded that action under superior orders could be used as mitigation.

Fatal Error

Sergeant Renji Sasakura demonstrating how he executed
Lieutenant DeLand Croze Kneeling is 2nd Lt Morris Forkosch,
trial investigator; to rear is Colonel Michinori Nakamura
(Photo from National Archives)

The following sentences, as modified by the review board, were handed down:

Colonel Michinori Nakamura, the man responsible for ordering and witnessing the execution, was sentenced to death by hanging. The sentence was approved.

Sergeant Renji Sasakura, who executed a member of the crew, was sentenced to death by hanging. His sentence was reduced to twenty years confinement at hard labor. He received an additional three years confinement at hard labor by an Australian court for his participation in the execution of an airman in Northern Celebes.

Sergeant Koshin Ichijo, who executed a member of the crew, was sentenced to death by hanging. His sentence was reduced to twenty years confinement at hard labor.

Private Fumiyuki Kazato was sentenced to death by firing squad for stabbing a prisoner who was already in the grave but thought to be still alive. His sentence was reduced to twenty years confinement at hard labor.

Lieutenant Kotaro Kamisuki, who attended the execution and ordered Private Kazato to stab a prisoner already in the grave, was sentenced to life in prison at hard labor. His sentence was approved.

Sergeant Major Shigeo Ichihashi, who guarded and blindfolded the men and then led them to the grave, was sentenced to confinement for life at hard labor. His sentence was reduced to fifteen years confinement at hard labor. He received an additional sentence of six years confinement at hard labor by an Australian court for beheading an airman in Northern Celebes.

Sergeant Kazuaki Okazaki, who guarded and blindfolded the men and then led them to the grave, was sentenced to life at hard labor. His sentence was reduced to fifteen years confinement at hard labor.

All sentences, including the hanging of Colonel Nakamura, were ordered to be carried out at Sugamo Prison in Tokyo.

Two other perpetrators, Major Toshitake Odamura and Warrant Officer Kunio Matsumoto, died before they could be brought to justice.

The guards from the 2nd Army Jail who executed two members of the crew were never identified.

The men sentenced to hard labor at Sugamo Prison in Tokyo did not serve more than ten years of their sentence and some served even less. When the occupying forces left Japan in 1952, the prison was turned over to the control of the Japanese who paroled many of the prisoners. In December, 1958, the prison was closed and all remaining prisoners were paroled.

EPILOGUE

The Survivors

DALE HUNT DID NOT REMEMBER much about the six hour flight back to Tawi-Tawi after he was picked up by the rescue plane. The morphine given to him by the crew of the rescue plane put him in a deep sleep and out of pain. He woke up for a minute or two while he was being transported to the ship and into the operating room. He knew the doctors were talking to him, he heard their voices, but he couldn't understand what they were saying.

In the middle of the night, he started screaming. The shark was coming at him, and he knew it would pull him under water again. The corpsman walked over to his bunk in sick bay, shook him awake, and turned on his bunk light. Dale saw that his right arm was bandaged from the elbow to the tips of his fingers. Only then did he realize that his left arm was gone. The corpsman sedated him with an injection of Nembutal.

During the time Hunt remained on the Pokomoke, he was unable to use his right hand. The squadron commander, Lieutenant Commander Bob Harper, arranged to have men from the squadron stay with Hunt by his bedside. They wrote letters for him, helped him change positions in the bed, and even helped feed and bathe him.

On June 21, 1945, both Dale Hunt and Lyle Bumpas were flown to Palawan Island in the Philippines where Seabees had built facilities to support patrol aircraft. The following day the men were flown to a hospital ship, USS Refuge (AH-11), for further treatment. The surgeons on the Refuge amputated parts of Hunt's badly damaged index finger and little finger on his only remaining hand. Unable to move his fingers, he was flown to a naval hospital in Mare Island, California. He underwent several operations to repair nerves and flexor tendons followed by months of physical and occupational therapy to make his right hand usable.

Eleven months after his injury, Hunt was honorably discharged from the navy on May 17, 1946. He collected $170 in pay and $119 for travel back to Kokomo, Indiana. After a few months, he managed to find full time employment with Stellite Division, a wrought iron operations plant in Kokomo, as a metal sorter. He was married and had a son, Dale Aaron Hunt, Jr. In July 1966, at age 40, Hunt was hospitalized again for injuries sustained in a fatal explosion at the plant. Dale recovered and continued his employment there until his retirement. He and his wife moved to Sanford, Florida, where he remained until his death on June 30, 2001, age 75.

In the mid 1980s, Dale Hunt had enjoyed a reunion with Daulton Stephenson in Tennessee. It was the first time they had seen each other since 1945. They spent a few days together, telling and retelling the story of the attack on their plane and the shark incident. Neither of them had been in contact with Lyle Bumpas, but managed to find him and spoke with him by telephone.

Daulton Stephenson was the only one of the three survivors who was not physically injured although he was suffering from exposure, dehydration and mental and physical exhaustion by the time he was rescued. He was sent back to the U.S. and was given thirty days recuperation leave. After his leave, he reported to the Naval Air Station Alameda, California, for temporary duty and was honorably discharged from the Navy in December, 1945.

Stephenson returned to farming, a life he had known since he was a child. He also worked at the Milan Arsenal and for Owens Corning. He and his wife, Jewel, raised two daughters. He lived a good life, active in his community and his church. Daulton died from heart problems and respiratory complications on July 18, 1992, at age 70.

Lyle Bumpas arrived back onboard the USS Pokomoke after his rescue on June 7, 1945. He was examined by the medical staff and found to be exhausted, dehydrated, and sunburned, as well as suffering from the

Daulton Stephenson and Dale Hunt in Mercer, Tennessee
(Courtesy of Donna Stephenson Dennison)

third degree burns and shell fragment wounds in his legs. He was mentally confused as a result of shock and the morphine administered in the rescue aircraft. The staff started treatment of his infected wounds and burns before transferring him to a navy hospital ship, USS Refuge (AH-11), for further care. By the end of June, he was in the Navy Hospital in Mare Island, California, where he received skin grafts for the burns on his leg. He remained there until declared fit for duty on August 17, 1945. He was then transferred to Memphis, Tennessee, and after twenty-three days leave received an honorable discharge from the navy.

The next couple of years were not easy for Lyle who was still mentally recovering and experiencing frightening flash backs. He went through a divorce and then received the shocking news that his friends on the plane had been either shot and killed or beheaded by the Japanese.

Slowly, his life improved. He remarried and had three children. Lyle developed into a man of many talents and interests. He raced motorcycles, was a butcher, sold real estate, had a business selling satellite dishes and another as heavy equipment contractor, according to his son Doug Bumpas. Doug said he was a wonderful father and great guy who made friends with everyone he came in contact with.

For the last twenty years of his life, Lyle worked for the Ford Motor Company as an electrician. He died of cancer on May 3, 1991, at age 65.

Lyle and Pat Bumpas
(Courtesy of Doug Bumpas)

Acknowledgements

I OWE A HUGE DEBT of gratitude to the many people who have helped me with this story. Especially to the family members of the crew who generously shared copies of photographs, letters, stories, and memorabilia of their loved ones. Their efforts helped me to get to know the members of the crew. I apologize if I have left anyone out.

Betty Morris, who found a suitcase in the trash containing photographs and documents pertaining to the event along with personal artifacts of Ensign Lewis Wheeler. Betty's son Tom Bunton, who preserved the suitcase and kept the items safe and intact. Without Betty and Tom, this story would not have been told.

Professor Gloria Stansberry, Ph.D., who took on the huge task of both editor and mentor for this first time writer. She improved the book with her ideas, her insights, and her confidence in me to tell the story. Thank you, Gloria.

Nancy Riikonen for her editing assistance and her support in helping me get this project through to the end.

Sally Olander of Sydney, Australia, my wonderful research buddy, who cheered me on at each new finding and shared her own successful research efforts to locate the last resting place of her beloved cousin, John Whitworth, a member of the Z Special Unit who gave his life trying to find the missing crew. There were times the research was so difficult and frustrating, I might have given it up were it not for Sally, right there by my side—half a world away, always providing support and guidance.

The late Jim Carter of West Covina, California, grand nephew of crewmember John Igoe. Jim researched this event over a span of several years and generously shared his findings with me.

Those wonderful research librarians who dug up information I would never have been able to find. Debbie Bloom of Columbia, S.C. researched the family of Marshall Hicks. Melissa Hicks of Brazil, Indiana researched the family of Donald Pell. Susan Daily, of the Wells County Public Library, helped me identify Kenny Crow by finding his photograph in an old high school yearbook. You librarians are amazing and always willing to give of your time to help others. Thank you.

Richard Garcia who has a large collection of items of his brother Joe Harvey Garcia. He scanned documents for days and photographed the things that wouldn't fit in the scanner. He interviewed Joe's buddies and sent along their stories. He shared his brother with me and allowed me to get to know Joe.

The late Maryanne Huls Dardarian, sister of Owen Huls, provided photographs and stories of her beloved brother even though it was very difficult for her to relive the painful memories. She worked through the pain to make sure her brother would not be forgotten. In gratitude for telling her brother's story, she left me his burial flag, a portrait taken in 1945 in San Diego, and his medals: the Silver Star, Purple Heart and Air Medal. Those artifacts will go to an appropriate museum. Thank you, Marianne, your brother was a hero and we hope he will never be forgotten.

Deni Halterman for arranging my visits to Maryanne Huls Dardarian, assisting with the visits and delivering the gifts from Marianne. Thanks Deni, without your help, visits to Maryanne would have been next to impossible.

Doug, Tim and Christy, the children of survivor Lyle Bumpas, shared photographs and wonderful stories of their father.

Donna Stephenson Dennison sent photos and an extensive newspaper article about her father, Daulton Stephenson.

Donna Bradburn, niece of Kenneth Crow, sent a large collection of photos and letters. She also sent a four page letter, hand written by Junior

Eichhorn, cousin and best friend of Kenneth, explaining what a wonderful person Kenny was.

Jean Eggleston, niece of Lewis Wheeler, gave me photos, stories, and his military ID card. It is obvious that this family's love and respect for their late uncle "the all American golden boy" is alive and well.

Melanie Mattsen and Katherine Croze, nieces of DeLand Croze and Nancy Doherty, the daughter of his widow, provided a collection of family photographs and stories.

Maurine Unrath sent photos and stories of her "Uncle Eddie", Edward Calhoun. She helped me identify him from the crew photograph.

Elaine Crafton and her daughters Joyce and Kim provided photos of their uncles, Charles Moorfield and his brother Alva.

Patricia Pell provided photographs of her father Donald Pell, a crew member of the USS Pokomoke who rode along with the crew of the PBM-5 on their last fateful patrol. Donald's nephews, Judge Robert Pell and Doctor Donald Pell, also sent along their memories of him.

Bill McKeown, former navy pilot and retired airline captain, for his technical assistance dealing with the PBM-5 aircraft.

The late Charlie Young, who shared an entire collection of photographs taken on board the USS Pokomoke during the war. He gave us the only photo we have of his best friend, Robert Jezewski.

WWII historian and documentary maker, John Schindler of Brisbane, Australia, who is filming the Australian side of this story, generously shared his work and ideas with me. Cheers, mate.

Australian WWII Z Special Unit veteran, Henry Fawkes, who risked his life to go behind enemy lines to search for the missing crew. His description of Operation Raven was so vivid, I felt like I was right there with him. I salute you, Henry.

Harumi Sakaguchi of Japan, who researched the post war location of Tokujiro Kato, a friendly Japanese interpreter, who treated the captive crewmen like gentlemen in the midst of a brutal environment. *Domo arigato* to both Harumi and Tokujiro.

Francis Crociata of Saint Leo University in Florida, who arranged for me to give a presentation of this story at the university and whose warm friendship and support have always been there through the years.

The late Clark Duane Roush, a co-pilot in Del Croze's squadron. Duane wrote and preserved stories of this incident years ago when it was still fresh in people's minds. And thanks to Duane's son, Steve Roush, who sent some wonderful photos of his father and crew.

Shean, Stephanie, Dan, and Skip, members of my writers critique group, who helped steer me in the right direction in those early struggling days.

Staff of National Personnel Records Center, St Louis, Missouri, for their assistance in making copies of the service records of each man on the plane.

NOTES

Chapter 1: Near Lalombi, Celebes, Dutch Indies
Listening for the rescue plane: War Diary, Patrol Bombing Squadron 20, 24 April to 25 July 1945, p. 22.
"Jezewski died last night": USS Pokomoke (AV 9), letter Pers-53210 to Secretary of the Navy, June 27, 1945.

Chapter 2: Selecting the Crew
Owen Huls arrived at the U.S. Navy's Banana River base: Owen D. Huls, Military Service Record, U.S. Navy Transfer Directive, November 1, 1944.
Lou Wheeler fresh from flight school: Diploma, Lewis A. Wheeler, Naval Air Training Center, Pensacola, Florida, October 3, 1944.
He had lived in a variety of places: Jean Eggleston, interview, November 21, 2013.
Later he lived for a time in Arcadia: Debra Bloom, written interview, August 13, 2009.
Marshall Hicks married Betty Belcher: Marriage Certificate, State of South Carolina, October 9, 1944.
"I rebuilt the engine on my 1937 Plymouth": Junior Eichhorn, personal letter to author, April 10, 2012.
"Tomorrow we're going on a simulated 12 hour patrol….": Lewis A. Wheeler, Aviator's Flight Log Book, November 29, 1944.
Description of PBM-5 Mariner: Hoffman, Richard A., *The Fighting Flying Boat: A History of the Martin PBM Mariner*, 2004, pp. 9-11.
Joe Garcia got the prized bow turret gun position: Naval Air Station Banana River, Florida, Combat Air Crew Battle Record, January 4, 1945.

Chapter 3: San Diego, California
Del Croze found he was eligible to stay at the Del Coronado Hotel: Charles Marion, personal letter to Henry Rink, June 7, 1996.

Hicks and his wife Betty found a room in a home at 5141 Marlborough Drive: H. B. Atkinson, correspondence from U.S. Navy Casualty Section, August 11, 1948.

In early February, Croze, Wheeler, Stephenson, Bumpas and Huls picked up a brand new PBM-5 Mariner, Bureau Number 59073: Lewis A. Wheeler, Aviators Flight Log Book, February 13, 1945.

Del Croze, wearing his normal lieutenant bars on one collar and a chaplain's cross on the other, entertained his fellow officers with humorous moral advice: Marion, June 7, 1996.

Chapter 4: Kaneohe Bay, Territory of Hawaii
Del Croze taxied the plane away from Coronado Island....: Lewis A. Wheeler, Aviators Flight Log Book, April 5, 1945.

Lou Wheeler...estimated flying time to be just over 16 hours: Ibid.

The seaplane base had been in existence since 1940: The Navy Department Library, Building the Navy's Bases in World War II 1940-1946, p. 416.

Igoe approved to join Croze's crew: F. E. Bardwell, Commander Fleet Air Wing TWO, letter to DeLand J. Croze, April 29, 1945.

"I expect our flight to Johnston Atoll will take us five and a half hours....: Lewis A. Wheeler, Aviators Flight Log Book, May 9, 1945.

Chapter 5: Hawaii to Tawi-Tawi
Croze landed the plane and taxied to ... where the seaplane lanes had been dredged: The Navy Department Library, Building the Navy's Bases in World War II 1940-1946, p. 417.

Garcia found an old sock abandoned on the beach and filled it with sea shells....They would be found later among his possessions when they cleaned out his locker: Joe H. Garcia, Military Service Record, Inventory of Personal Effects, June 9, 1945.

The plane took off early the morning of May 10th for Kwajalein atoll: Lewis A. Wheeler, Aviators Flight Log Book, May 10, 1945.

In the morning, they took off at 0800 for a nine hour flight to Saipan: Ibid.

Vice-Admiral Chuichi Nagumo committed suicide: William Stewart, *Admirals of the World: A Biographical Dictionary, 1500-Present*, 2009, p. 230.

Among the wounded was Hollywood actor Lee Marvin: Dwayne Epstein, *Lee Marvin: Point Blank*, 2013. pp. 50-51.

Monday, March 14th, the crew flew to Jinamoc Island: Lyle Bumpas, Aviators Flight Log Book, March 14, 1945.

"No Japanese–no Japanese!" the Asians yelled. "We Filipinos...We friends!": memoirs of Lyle Bumpas as told by his son Doug Bumpas, undated.

Navy brought in 45 Quonset huts for berthing with additional...: The Navy Department Library, Building the Navy's Bases in World War II, History of the Bureau of Yards and Docks and the Civil Engineer Corps 1940-1946, p.382.

On May 17th the crew departed ... for their final destination of Tawi-Tawi: Lewis A. Wheeler, Aviators Flight Log Book, May 17, 1945.

Chapter 6: Tawi-Tawi, Philippine Islands
...we have 15 PBM-5 Mariner aircraft manned by 61 officers and 171 combat air crewmen: War Diary, Patrol Bombing Squadron 20, May 1945, pp. 1-2.

"Charles, I'm very sorry to tell you your brother, Gunners Mate First Class Alva Moorfield, was killed a week ago at Okinawa": Elaine Crafton, telephone interview, February 24, 2010.

By 0730 the plane was ...flying southwest toward Sandakan Harbor. Del Croze was the pilot and Lieutenant Rumrey sat in the co-pilot seat: War Diary, Patrol Bombing Squadron 20, May 1945, p.8.

Croze and Rumrey both spotted the two black motorboats leaving Nunuyan Darat: Ibid.

The rest of the afternoon Croze assisted six PT boats: Ibid.

"We've received reports that the Japs have a bomber at Sandakan that they fly every night at dusk": Ibid., p. 9.

Chapter 7: Attack on Sandakan Harbor
At 0745, they rendezvoused with two PT boats...:War Diary, p. 9
The wing collapsed just as Croze released a 250 pound bomb...: Ibid.
With a change in orders from the squadron, they set a course for Darvel Bay: Ibid.
The two planes...take part in a major attack on Sandakan Harbor led by Lieutenant Richard Monahon and his squadron of nine PT boats: Ibid., p. 10.
A group of 25 Japanese Marines...had arrived in Sandakan to man the suicide boats: Robert J. Buckley, *At Close Quarters: PT Boats in the United States Navy*,
1962. p. 21.

Chapter 8: First Long War Patrol
Garcia was just five feet two inches tall and weighed 123 pounds: Joe H. Garcia, Military Service Record, Physical Examination Report, January 14, 1944.
He would put the bully in his place: Richard Garcia, interview, March 12, 2012.
Igoe was born in Ireland.... John P. Igoe, Military Service Record, Application for Enlistment, April 14, 1942.
The skipper had told him they would be taking two riders along: War Diary, Patrol Bombing Squadron 20, June 1945, p.6.
"The Seventh Fleet Air Command has ordered us to scour the east coast of Borneo": Patrol Bombing Squadron 20, Narrative, Tawi-Tawi Operations, 25 April to 25 July 1945, pp. 22-24.
Stephenson loved navigation and often helped the navigator with his job: Dan Morris, "Sacrifices Speak for WWII's Warriors," *The Jackson Sun*, Jackson, Tennessee, May 30, 2010, pp. A1 & A6.
Tapping his breast pocket to make sure he had his New Testament: Ibid.

Chapter 9: Along the East Coast of Borneo

"Looks like two Japanese merchants with a gunboat escort": War Patrol Bombing Squadron 20, Narrative, Tawi-Tawi Operations, 25 April - 25 July 1945, pp. 22-24.

Shrapnel from the explosion hit Robert Jezewski...blowing off his right foot: Ibid.

The concussion blew Ensign Hicks out of the plane: Ibid.

Bumpas burned by scalding hot hydraulic oil.....: Ibid.

Two major fuel tanks lost, leaving only enough fuel for two hours flight time: Ibid.

"QAL *(I am landing at)* SEA 00.00 degrees 119.20 E": Ibid.

Chapter 10: Near Lalombi, Celebes, Dutch East Indies

"There were eight...soldiers carrying rifles...": War Patrol Bombing Squadron 20, narrative, pp. 22- 24.

Japanese Navy Lieutenant Yoshio Araki had arrived in the early morning with twelve armed soldiers from their small garrison in Donggala, 20 miles to the north: Ibid.

PBM-5 Mariner under the command of Lieutenant White had been searching throughout the night: Ibid.

The four unarmed men ran down the beach: Ibid.

The men ran into the mangrove swamp, crouched down in water up to their necks and covered their heads with palm fronds: Ibid.

Used three fallen coconut palms for a raft: Ibid.

Two planes from Tawi-Tawi were spending a second night looking for them: Ibid.

Chapter 11: Under Attack

A slug penetrated Hicks' left foot and another shattered his left leg bone at the knee: War Trial Records, United States of America vs. Michinori Nakamura et al., January 24, 1947, Report of Activities. p. 1.

The soldiers loaded the men onto the truck: Emory C. Smith, Letter Report of Chief Prosecutor to Chief Legal Section, Supreme Commander for the Allied Powers, Manila, 15 February 1947.

Kenny Crow smelled the rice and decided he didn't want it: Ibid.

There was just enough light to see the plane as Huls began to swim ashore: Ibid.

Huls shouted as loudly as he could: Ibid.

Two rescue planes spent the day looking without success: Patrol Bombing Squadron 20, Narrative, Tawi-Tawi Operations, 25 April to 25 July 1945, p. 22-24.

Chapter 12: Rescue at Sea

At 0630 hours, Forsha and Saylor took off from Tawi-Tawi: Patrol Bombing Squadron 20, Narrative, pp. 22-24.

Hunt, and Bumpas caught a morning breeze that carried them westward: Ibid.

Ordnanceman Wally Pasco sees the beached plane...: Jim Carter, interview with Wally Pasco, June 3, 2009.

The two planes...decided to fly inland to look for survivors there: Patrol Bombing Squadron 20, Narrative, Tawi-Tawi Operations, 25 April-25 July 1945, p. 2.

AMM2 W. C. Moore, the crew chief on Morgan Saylor's plane sees the men: Clark Duane Roush, Aviation, Air Progress Aviation Review. "PBM to the Rescue," *Aviation: Air Progress Aviation Review*, Spring 1979, pp. 44-51.

Forsha sees numerous reefs making landing dangerous: Ibid.

Saylor fears being dead in the water with Japanese soldiers in the area: Ibid.

He swam about 15 feet when he spotted the fin coming at him: Ibid.

Morgan Saylor sends his co-pilot to help with IV's: Ibid.

"I've never stuck a needle in anyone....": Ibid.

Most of the flesh and tendons in that arm had been torn away by the shark: War Diary, Patrol Bombing Squadron 20, June 194, p. 3.

Hunt and Bumpas were flown to a hospital ship...: Ibid.

Bumpas sent home for rest: Ibid.

Croze and his three crewmen were… driven from Donggala to a larger Japanese garrison in the town of Palu, twenty miles northeast: Smith, 15 February 1947.

They locked the door and gave the medical staff strict orders that Hicks was not to be given either food or medical attention: Ibid.

The local Indonesian doctor begged the Japanese to allow him to treat Hicks but they refused and threatened him with death if he disobeyed their orders: Ibid.

Chapter 13: Operation Raven, the Search for the Missing Crew

The Squadron Commander sent a request for help to the Allied Intelligence Bureau (AIB) on Morotai Island: Patrol Bombing Squadron 20, Narrative, Tawi-Tawi Operations, 25 April to 25 July 1945, p. 24.

The Z Special Unit of the Australian Army takes on the search: Services Reconnaissance Department, Morotai Island, Indonesia, Operational Report, June 23, 1945, p. 2.

With official permission from General MacArthur, the American squadron picked up the Z Special team from Morotai Island and flew them to Tawi-Tawi: Ibid.

The dispensary staff buried him the next morning in the hospital cemetery with a marker that said "American Pilot": Smith, 15 February 1947.

McFerren-Rogers had his team… ready to launch their raft: War Diary, Patrol Bombing Squadron 20, June 1945, p. 10.

The prop wash was so strong it overturned the raft: Ibid.

The following day, the resupplied team… returned to the area south of Croze's beached PBM-5, Ibid.

Plans to stay ashore at least one night and expand the search area: Ibid., p. 10.

Major Tony Gluth was the newly assigned leader and McFerran-Rogers would assist. Corporals Leahy, Fawkes, Hopkins and Private Whitworth were added to the team: Services Reconnaissance Department, Operational Report, June 23, 1945, p. 2.

Corporal Philpott had to drop out: Henry Fawkes, member of Raven II party, telephone interview, May 21, 2012.

Lieutenant Saylor delivered the team to an area north of the beached plane: War Diary, Patrol Bombing Squadron 20, June 1945, p. 10.

When Australians threaten to force natives to return with them, they burst into tears: Fawkes, telephone interview, May 21, 2012.

The team began a three hour trek and finally arrived at the village of Sodi at 1400: Ibid.

The team observed a cart pulled by a water buffalo on the opposite side of the river: Ibid.

One of the men in the cart appeared to be wearing a U. S Navy dungaree shirt: Ibid.

Gluth takes Roestan and Whitworth to other side of river: Ibid.

The men sleep on the river bank, awaiting morning arrival of the PBM-5: Ibid.

Corporal Henry Fawkes attempts to rescue McFerran-Rogers: Ibid.

All the men, except for Private John Whitworth, ran toward the rubber raft: Ibid.

John Whitworth tried to evade the enemy but was captured: Ibid.

Chapter 14: In Custody of the Kempei Tai

Colonel Michinori Nakamura asked the men to be transferred to his command: War Trial Records, United States of America vs. Michinori Nakamura et al. January 24, 1947, p. 45.

The men went by truck, then by sea, and by truck again to reach their destination of Singkang: Smith, 15 February 1947.

An eye witness, Dr. Stamford Rampen, a veterinary surgeon, observes arrival: War Trial Records, United States of America vs. Michinori Nakamura et al., January 24, 1947, p. 91.

Del Croze had a four or five day growth of beard and appeared to be in good health: Ibid.

All the men appeared to be in good health: Ibid.

They tied the men and put them in separate rooms: Ibid.

Col. Nakamura asks Maj. Odamura to prepare questions for the Americans: Ibid.

Sergeant Tokujiro Kato was born and raised in southern California: Ibid. p. 423.

Kato dismissed the guard, untied Croze, and asked him to be seated: Ibid. p. 421.

"Well, I was born in Brawley, California,...": Ibid. p. 423.

One by one, Crow, Garcia and Calhoun were interrogated by Kato: Ibid.

They discovered there was another American in the jail: Smith, 15 February 1947

They also became friends with a young Indonesian man: War Trial Records, United States of America vs. Michinori Nakamura et al. Report of Activities, November 7, 1946, pp.1-4.

Isa hated the Japanese and during an escape attempt killed a Kempei Tai guard: Ibid.

Once a week the American prisoners were taken for a walk: Ibid.

An attached length of rope was tied around their ankles: Ibid.

The local people noted how every week the Americans appeared to be weaker: Ibid.

Veterinary surgeon, Stamford Rampen saw Joe Garcia one day in the yard outside the jail: War Trial Records, United States of America vs. Michinori Nakamura et al., January 24, 1947, pp. 92-94.

Rampen saw Garcia standing in the yard: Ibid.

Colonel Nakamura decided to use one of the American prisoners for propaganda: Ibid.

"I can't tell one from the other ...Use the small one.": Ibid.

"After dinner... they handed out a photograph to each guest...": Ibid.

An Indonesian boy was kneeling by Garcia's side....: Ibid., p. 94.

Chapter 15: The Execution

On July 27th, Colonel Nakamura sent his second in command to see Lieutenant Colonel Ishiro: War Trial Records, United States of America vs. Michinori Nakamura, et al. January 24, 1947, p. 296.

"...He whispered to me that we could just dispose of them": Ibid.

Odamura returned to visit with Lieutenant Colonel Ishiro: Ibid. p. 297.

Odamura called Warrant Officer Matsumoto and directed him to write the execution plan: Ibid.

It was clear that the men suspected what was coming: Ibid.

Matsumoto and four guards marched the American prisoners to the Second Army jail: Ibid.

Matsumoto left two of his sergeants, Shigeo Ichihashi and Kazuaki Okazaki to guard the prisoners: Ibid.

Standing around the grave were...: Ibid.

Fumiyuki Kazato, arrived with rain coats for the officers: Ibid.

"Send the big one first": Ibid.

Sergeant Major Ichihashi blind folded Croze and led him to the grave: Ibid. p. 82.

Sasakura drew his sword and poured water on the blade...: Ibid., p. 77.

Matsumoto had planned to use only Kempei Tai soldiers: Ibid. p. 83.

Chapter 16: End of the War

Flight Lieutenant Martin O'Shea was led to the mass grave by Doctor Djanharajah Yenie, a surgeon from the local leper hospital: War Trial Records, United States of America vs. Michinori Nakamura et al. Report of Activities, October 8, 1948, p. 1.

The property owner had discovered the freshly dug grave: Ibid.

The bodies were exhumed from the mass grave: Ibid. p. 4.

The bodies were buried in a temporary national cemetery in Calcutta: Ibid. pp. 1-2.

During the trial review a motion was made to dismiss the charges against...: Trial Review United States of America vs. Michinori Nakamura et al. December 9, 1947, p. 30.

Colonel Michinori Nakamura sentenced to death by hanging: Ibid. p. 32.

Sergeant Renji Sasakura sentence was reduced to 20 years: Ibid.

He received an additional 3 years confinement at hard labor by an Australian court: National Archives of Australia, War Crimes Trial, Summary of Proceedings, Trial of Sgt Sasakura, Rinji, Series AWM54, 1946-1946.

Sergeant Koshin Ichijo'sentence was reduced to 20 years confinement at hard labor: Trial Review United States of America vs. Michinori Nakamura, December 9, 1947, p. 32.

Private Fumiyuki Kazato was sentenced to death by firing squad: Ibid.

Lieutenant Kotaro Kamisuki was sentenced to life in prison at hard labor: Ibid.

Sergeant Major Shigeo Ichihashi's sentence was reduced: Ibid.

He received an additional sentence for beheading an airman in Northern Celebes: National Archives of Australia, War Crimes Trial, Summary of Proceedings, Trial of Sgt. Maj. Ichihashi, Shigeo, Series AWM54, 1946-1946.

Sergeant Kazuaki Okazaki sentence was reduced: Trial Review United States of America vs. Michinori Nakamura, December 9, 1947, p. 30.

All sentences were ordered to be carried out at Sugamo Prison in Tokyo: Ibid., p. 4.

The prison was turned over to the Japanese and closed...: John L. Ginn, Sugamo Prison, Tokyo, "An account of the Trial and Sentencing of Japanese War Criminals in 1948, by a U.S. Participant," 1992, p. 242.

Epilogue: The Survivors

"Hunt was hospitalized again for injuries sustained in a fatal explosion": *Kokomo Morning Times*, July 20, 1966. Also, *Kokomo Tribune*, "Stellite Blast," July 28, 1966.

"He [Hunt] and his wife moved to Sanford, Florida, where he remained until his death...": *Kokomo Tribune*, June 24, 2001, p. A2.

"Stephenson returned to farming...": Interview with Donna Stephenson Dennison, May 6, 2012.

"The next couple of years were not easy for Lyle...Slowly his life improved"...: Interview with Greg Bumpas, December 12, 2010.

BIBLIOGRAPHY

Books
Buckley, Robert J. *At Close Quarters: PT Boats in the United States Navy.* Washington DC: Naval Institute Press, 1962.
Epstein, Dwayne. *Lee Marvin: Point Blank.* Tucson, Az.: Shaffner Press, 2013.
Ginn, John L. *Sugamo Prison, Tokyo: An Account of the Trial and Sentencing of Japanese War Criminals in 1948, by a U.S. Participant.* Jefferson, N.C.: McFarland, 1962.
Hoffman, Richard A. *The Fighting Flying Boat: A History of the Martin PBM Mariner.* Annapolis, Md., 2004.
Stewart, William. *Admirals of the World: A Biographical Dictionary, 1500-Present.* Jefferson, N.C.: McFarland, 2009.

Internet Document
The Navy Department Library. Building the Navy's Bases in World War II. History of the Bureau of Yards and Docks and the Civil Engineering Corps 1940-1946. http://www.history.navy.mil/library/online/buildbaseswwii/bbwwiicontents.htm

Documents
Aviators Flight Log Books of Wheeler, Lewis and Bumpas, Lyle.
Bumpas, Greg. *Memoirs of Lyle Bumpas*, as told by his son Doug Bumpas, undated.
Military Service Records of men on the aircraft. National Archives Branch, St Louis, Mo.
Naval Air Station Banana River, Florida, Combat Air Crew Battle Record, January 4, 1945.
Patrol Bombing Squadron 20, Narrative, Tawi-Tawi Operations, 25 April to 25 July 1945.
Services Reconnaissance Department, Morotai Island, Indonesia: Operational Report June 23, 1945.

War Crimes Trials: Summary of Proceedings. Trial of Sgt. Sasakura, Sgt. Rinji and Sgt.Maj. Shigeo Ichihashi. Series AWM54, 1946-1946. National Archives of Australia.

War Diary – Patrol Squadron 20, 24 April to 25 July 1945.

War Diary – Patrol Squadron 20, May 1945.

War Diary – Patrol Squadron 20, June 1945.

War Trial Records: United States of America vs. Michinori Nakamura, et al. January 24, 1947. Record Group 331, Box 1580, National Archives, Washington DC

Magazine

Roush, Clark Duane. "PBM to the Rescue." *Aviation Air Progess: Aviation Review*, Spring 1979.

Newspaper

Morris, Dan. "Sacrifices Speak for WWII's Warriors." *The Jackson Sun [Tenn.]*, May 30, 2010.

Obituary – Dale Hunt. *Kokomo Tribune*, June 24, 2001, p. A2.

"Stellite Blast." *Kokomo Morning Times*, July 20, 1966.

"Stellite Blast." *Kokomo Tribune*, July 28, 1966.

Letters

Bardwell, F. E., Commander Fleet Air Wing TWO, to DeLand J. Croze, April 29, 1945.

Crow, Kenneth J., to his sister Helen Crow Robinson, May 7, 1945.

Eichhorn, Junior, to the author, April 10, 2012.

Marion, Charles, to Henry Rink, June 7, 1996.

Smith, Emory C. Letter Report to Chief Prosecutor to Chief Legal Section, Supreme Commander for the Allied Powers, Manila, February 15, 1947.

USS Pokomoke (AV 0) letter Pers-53210 to Secretary of the Navy, June 27, 1945.